A WEALTH OF INFORMATION
AT YOUR FINGERTIPS

Less than thirty years ago UNIVAC I, the first mass-produced electronic computer, cost a million dollars and filled a huge room. Today the Timex/Sinclair 1000 sells for less than $100, fits in your briefcase or handbag, and is just as powerful and far, far easier to use—if you know how.

Now this easy-to-understand handbook will teach you how to use your T/S 1000 at business or at home, for profits, savings, ease, efficiency, education, and computer game-playing fun. You will find out how it works, what all its different parts do, how to program it, and how to expand its possibilities with accessories. And this is just a small part of what you'll discover and enjoy in this most invaluable guide to the new computer age.

Titles of Related Interest from MENTOR and SIGNET

THE
TIMEX®
PERSONAL COMPUTER MADE SIMPLE

A GUIDE TO THE TIMEX/SINCLAIR 1000

JOE CAMPBELL, JONATHAN D. SIMINOFF,
AND JEAN YATES

A SIGNET BOOK
NEW AMERICAN LIBRARY
TIMES MIRROR

ACKNOWLEDGMENTS

Our thanks to the following people for their contributions: Joel Klutch, who debugged and tested the programs and supplied valuable advice during rewrite; Joanne Clapp for her word-processing wizardry; Tom Bell of Addison-Wesley for his patience; and Tom Seccombe, who lent us a computer early on.

This book was planned, prepared, and produced by the Microcomputer Books Group of Addison-Wesley Publishing Company, Inc.

Ann Dilworth, Publisher and Vice-President
Thomas A. Bell, Sponsoring Editor
David Miller, Assistant Editor and Designer
Barbara Wood, Managing Editor

TIMEX® is a registered trademark of Timex Corporation

Photographs by Sharon A. Bazarian

Drawings by Marci Davis

Published by arrangement with Addison-Wesley Publishing Company

Contents

Preface

You've heard about the coming computer revolution. Now it's here, and the Timex/Sinclair 1000 gives you the opportunity to participate in it. This book is your introduction to the fast-paced world of high technology. Only a few years ago computers were the province of white-jacketed mathematicians who trained for years before they could work with machines the size of a warehouse. Now anybody with the time it takes to read this book can learn to use the Timex/Sinclair personal computer—the first computer to sell for less than $100 and one that's so small you can take it with you wherever you go.

Use the T/S 1000 to balance your checkbook, figure your taxes, or assess which bank will give you the best deal on a mortgage. It's both an educational tool and an entertaining toy. Hook it up to your TV and play games on it. Write programs for it—this book will show you how. But most important, the T/S will turn you into a budding computer scientist, ready to move on to bigger, more sophisticated equipment. The T/S 1000 uses BASIC, the most popular computer programming language in the world. After learning about BASIC from this book, you'll be ready to program computers for any number of purposes. This is a computer that *everyone* can use.

Chapter 1 explains computers—what they are made of and how they work. Chapter 2 launches you on your programming career. In it you'll learn the basics of BASIC and how to write and troubleshoot programs.

By the time you've finished Chapter 3 and your first program, you can consider yourself a computer veteran. To learn how to store your program on tape, see Chapter 5. Are you a game player or do you want to be? Skip to Chapters 7 and 8. Planning to use the computer at home? Chapter 10 covers home uses, from checkbook balancing to figuring mortgage payments. Perhaps you're more interested in how you can best utilize your computer in the office. See Chapter 11 for details.

Finally, there are the appendixes—guides to computer accessories, add-on parts, and resources for finding out more about them. There is also a glossary, and another appendix which explains all the mysteries of the keyboard. A final appendix lists the T/S 1000's internal codes.

Tired of standing on the sidelines? Want to take part in the twenty-first century? *Turn the page . . .*

The Timex/Sinclair 1000 personal computer system

1

Getting Started

Computers are literal-minded, quiet, and obedient. They will do exactly what you tell them to do, as long as it is physically possible and they understand your instructions. But first you need to learn their special language.

Your Timex/Sinclair 1000 computer is an excellent tool to teach you how to use a computer. For that reason, this book is designed to be used with your T/S 1000 in front of you. For every point made, an example is presented; please try them all. Using a computer is like riding a bicycle, swimming, cooking, or throwing a Frisbee. Someone can start you in the right direction, but you can really learn only by doing.

INSTALLING YOUR COMPUTER

Clear a good-sized table and put your TV on it. A small black-and-white TV is best, but any kind will do. When you remove your new T/S 1000 from the box, you will find the following items.

The computer. As you've probably guessed, this is the object with the keyboard printed on the top. It contains four

Above: The power supply (left) is plugged into an outlet or extension cord; the end of the power supply cord goes into the hole on the computer marked 9V DC. *Below*: The antenna switch box connects to your TV set.

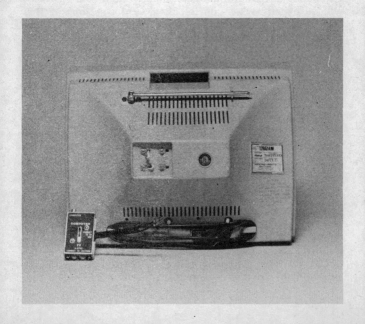

jack sockets on the left side. They are labeled TV, EAR, MIC, and 9V DC.

A power supply. This is a small, square box with a power cord built into it. Plug the power supply into a wall outlet or extension cord. Plug the end of the cord into the socket on the computer labeled 9V DC. Don't worry about plugging it into the wrong hole or touching the plug accidentally; no harm will be done, but the cord must be plugged into the 9V DC socket for the computer to operate.

An antenna switch box. This is a small metal box about 3″ × 2″ × 1″ with a short two-wire, flat cable coming out of one side, and a slide switch labeled COMPUTER and TV. Slide the switch to the COMPUTER position. Now check the rear of your TV. It should have two or four screws for antenna connectors. If the TV has its own antenna built in, the screws are probably near that antenna. Most TVs have two sets of screws, one set marked UHF the other marked VHF. The VHF antenna screws, which are for channels 2–13, are usually the lower pair. Unscrew the VHF antenna screws slightly, insert the U-shaped parts at the ends of the flat cable underneath the screws, and tighten. It doesn't matter which U connector goes under which screw, so long as they go under different ones and both of the screws are for VHF. If there are only two screws, they are probably for VHF, so just use these. If your TV has an internal/external antenna switch near the antenna screws, move it to the external position.

A video cable. This is a wire about 4 feet long, with a plug on each end. Plug either end into the socket labeled TV on the left side of the computer. Plug the other end into the antenna switch box. You will see a socket on one side, sticking out a bit, to accommodate the video cable.

A book. The book can serve as your reference manual. It is not, however, an ideal text for learning to use your T/S 1000. The book you are now reading was written especially for that purpose.

A 2-foot cable with plugs on each end. This is used when connecting your computer to a cassette tape recorder. Put it aside until you get to Chapter 5.

Your computer is now completely installed. Turn on your TV and wait until a picture appears. Turn the TV to Channel 2 or 3, whichever has a weaker station in your area. Turn the volume all the way down.

On the bottom of the computer you'll find a switch labeled ch 2 and ch 3. Select the switch position that matches the channel you selected on the TV.

Your TV screen should now be blank except for the lower left corner, where you should see a small black box with a K inside. (If you're using a color TV, there might be some color in the picture. If this annoys you, turn the color control off.) If you don't see the box, or if the picture is not stable, adjust the controls on your TV for the best picture. If the picture is still not satisfactory, try switching to the other channel. (If you are on 2, try 3, and vice versa; also try the channel switch on the bottom of your TV.) Here's a checklist for possible problems:

1. Make sure that the switch on the antenna switch box is set to COMPUTER.
2. If your TV has an internal/external antenna switch, try both positions.
3. Try disconnecting the TV's regular antenna.
4. If the television screen is lighted, but there is no K, try adjusting the vertical and horizontal hold on your TV. It is possible that the K is "hidden" below the bottom of the TV screen. If your TV receives local stations clearly, it will work with the computer.

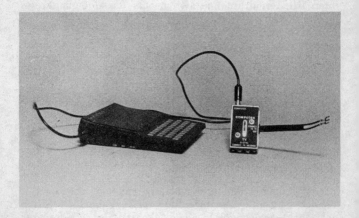

The video cable connects the computer and the antenna switch box.

5. If you have cable television, try disconnecting the cable. TV cables are sometimes connected inside the set; it is possible that you will have to use a TV that is not connected to cable.
6. Are both ends of the video cable plugged securely into their sockets? They should be secure enough not to slip out accidentally.
7. Is the computer plugged in? Check that the lead from the power supply is securely in its socket. Be sure that the power supply is plugged into a working socket.
8. Finally, try another TV. If you have one, a good-quality, small, black-and-white portable is best.
9. If nothing works, and the computer doesn't work with any television you try, take it back to the store and ask the clerk to try it. You may have received a defective unit.

I will assume that if you have reached this point, your TV now has a stable, blank screen with a K in the bottom left corner. Since your computer may require different settings than your favorite TV shows do, adjust the brightness and contrast to suit your tastes.

Now it's time to put your computer to work!

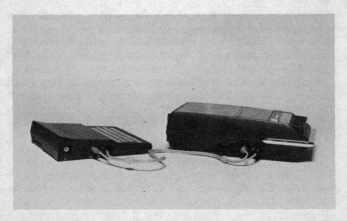

The other cable connects the computer to a cassette tape recorder (see Chapter 5).

2

Using Your
Timex/Sinclair 1000

The black box now on your screen is called a *cursor*. It indicates that the computer is waiting for you to give it a command. It also indicates where the next character will be printed on your TV. Look at the keyboard printed on the top of the computer. If you have ever used a typewriter, the arrangement of the keys will be familiar to you. Press the P. The word **PRINT** appears instead of the letter P, and the ▊K▊ inside the cursor has changed to an ▊L▊. Although the keyboard looks like a miniature typewriter, the keys function differently. Most of the keys have words directly above and below them and have words or symbols, along with a letter or number, directly on the keys.

When the ▊K▊ appears on the lower line, the computer is asking you to enter a *keyword*. A keyword is the most basic part of a computer command. When the computer expects a keyword, touching one of the letter keys (A–Z) makes the computer print the entire keyword written above the letter. So, when you touch P, **PRINT** appears. Try typing a P now that the ▊L▊ cursor is on the bottom line. This time, a P appears on the TV screen. The ▊L▊ cursor means that the computer expects something besides a keyword. The keywords written above the letters will print only if the ▊K▊

The Timex/Sinclair 1000 keyboard

cursor is on the screen. By the way, the Timex/Sinclair 1000 is designed to produce only capital letters.

Every key has something in red printed on it. When you press the **SHIFT** key and simultaneously press almost any other key, the red item on the key prints on the screen.

The red word on the key in the upper right corner, the 0 key, is **DELETE**. Hold down the **SHIFT** key and at the same time press **DELETE**. The letter P you previously typed disappears. **DELETE (SHIFT/0)** removes the letter or keyword immediately to the left of the cursor. Press **DELETE** again and the keyword **PRINT** disappears. If you have done all of this, you are now back at the beginning of the line, and the cursor is once again ▓. Press P again, and **PRINT** appears again. The cursor is now ▐.

Hold the **SHIFT** key down and press P once more. A double quotation mark (") , written in red on the P key, appears on the TV. Release **SHIFT**. Type the word HELLO. Notice that now, as you press the alphabetic keys, the alphabetic letters appear. Hold **SHIFT** down and press P again. Another quotation mark appears. The line should look like this:

PRINT "HELLO"

The key to the far right, on the third row down, is labeled **ENTER**. The computer will do nothing with your line until you press **ENTER**. Press **ENTER**. The word HELLO appears on the top left corner of your TV.

You just gave the computer the command to print the word HELLO on the TV screen. The computer always begins printing at the top of the screen. Your typing always appears at the bottom of the screen. The bottom line of the screen now shows 0/0. That is a *report code*, a message from the computer saying it encountered no problems doing what you asked. When a report code is displayed, it also serves as the ▓ cursor.

Now type **PRINT** and press **ENTER**. The HELLO at the top of the screen disappears. Entering a **PRINT** by itself prints a blank line. The usefulness of this will become apparent later.

Type **PRINT** "HELLO" again. Remember to press the P when the ▓ cursor is on the screen, and then **SHIFT**/P to get the quotation mark, then the letters H, E, L, L, and O, and then **SHIFT**/P for the last quotation mark. Don't press **ENTER** yet.

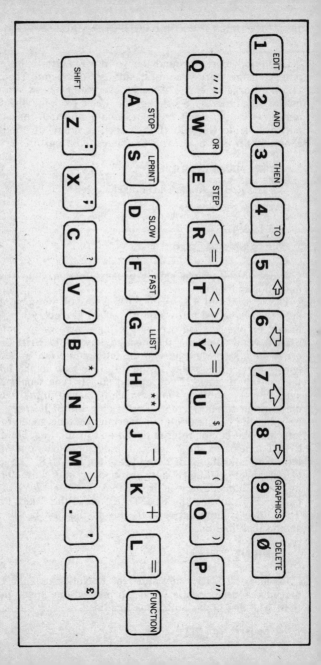

These are the operational symbols when the SHIFT key is pressed.

Quotation marks around the word HELLO tell the computer that the word was not meant as a command. The quotation marks mean "Accept everything between the quotation marks as a whole, and don't examine the contents." (That is, don't try to evaluate it.) Any characters may be inside the quotation marks. A group of "quoted" characters is called a *string*. Examples of strings are:

"MY NAME IS MUD"

"GOODBYE APRIL OLD FRIEND"

"!@#$%'%'&*(*"

"123.456"

"123+256=379"

These are all strings simply because they are enclosed in quotation marks.

The 5, 6, 7, and 8 keys on the top row of the computer's keyboard have red arrows on them. Just like everything else in red on the keyboard, you use these arrows by holding **SHIFT** while pressing the desired key. Hold **SHIFT** and press the 5 key, the one with the left arrow. Notice that the cursor moves one space to the left. It is now to the left of the quotation mark. If you looked closely, you would have seen that the quotation mark actually moved to the right to make room for the cursor. Try holding the **SHIFT** key and pressing the 8. The quotation mark moves one space to the left, and the cursor returns to the end of the line. Hold the **SHIFT** and press the 5 again. The cursor moves one space left. Now hold the **SHIFT** and press the **DELETE**. The letter O disappears. **DELETE** always removes one character (or keyword) immediately in front (that is, to the *left*) of the cursor. Still holding the **SHIFT** key, press the 5 key twice. The cursor is now between the E and the first L. The line should look like this:

PRINT "HE█LL"

Release the **SHIFT** key and type L. Notice that the L replaced the cursor while the cursor moved one space to the right. The line now should look like this:

PRINT "HEL█LL"

Type another L, then an O. The key in the lower right corner is labeled **SPACE**. The key next to it is marked with a black period and a red comma. Hold the **SHIFT** and press the comma key. Now release **SHIFT** and press the **SPACE** key. A blank space appears. Type an N, then an E. The line looks like this:

PRINT "HELLO, NE▉LL"

Now press **ENTER**. The line disappears and HELLO, NELL appears on the top left of the TV screen in place of the HELLO that was printed before. Notice that the position of the cursor on the line does not matter once you press **ENTER**, and the cursor is never printed as part of the line. Also, notice that the quotation marks are not printed. Notice that the Q key has two red quotation marks written on it. You have to use those double quotation marks if you want to use quotation marks within a string; these are **SHIFT**/Q. Try this:

PRINT "MARGARET SAID " "HELLO" " TO ME"

Something odd happened when you were typing that in, didn't it? When you reached the O of TO, you were at the end of the line; when you typed O, the line moved up one, and everything else went on the next line. A line on the TV screen holds only 32 characters, but as far as the computer is concerned, the lines may be any length. The computer will begin a new line when necessary. You may, of course, use as many lines as you like. Since the computer doesn't do anything until you type **ENTER**, do so now. The following line appears at the top of the TV screen:

MARGARET SAID 'HELLO' TO ME

Notice that the double quotation marks (**SHIFT**/Q) have been reduced to single quotation marks. The doubled quotation symbol is exclusively for the computer's internal use to prevent confusion about the location of the end of a string. When the computer executes your command to print the string, it will print only a single quotation mark.

The TV now has one line of writing at the top of the screen. Let's do some "housecleaning." To erase the line, give the clear screen command, **CLS**. **CLS** is written above

the V key. Since the ▨ cursor is currently displayed, touching the V key will print **CLS**. Try it, then press **ENTER**. The
screen becomes blank.

The individual letters cannot be typed when the ▨ cursor
is on the screen. In other situations (which you will encoun-
ter as you proceed through this book) you will be allowed
to type letters even if a keyword is required. Typing the individual letters (even though they *appear* to make up the
identical word) is not the same as typing one of the keywords. That is important to remember. If your typing is not
accepted by the T/S 1000, check to be sure you have used a
keyword.

Keywords are always typed with one key and can always
be erased by typing **DELETE** (**SHIFT**/O) once. In this book,
keywords are written in **bold type**.

Numbers, but not letters, may be typed at the beginning
of a line. Type this number:

100

Notice that the ▨ cursor is currently displayed. Touch the
P key, to make the word **PRINT** appear. The ▨ cursor is
now displayed. Now hold **SHIFT** and press P again, so that
a quotation mark (") appears. Type HELLO, followed by another quotation mark. The line should look like this.

100 **PRINT** "HELLO"

Now press **ENTER**.

The word HELLO is not printed on the screen. Instead,
the entire line 100 **PRINT** "HELLO" disappears from the
bottom of the screen and reappears at the top.

When a number is typed in front of a command, that
number is called a *line number*. Commands with line numbers are not executed immediately. The computer copies
the line and retains it.

The R key is labeled **RUN**. Press the R key. The word
RUN appears on the bottom line of the screen. Press **EN-
TER**.

The word HELLO now appears on the top line of the
screen. You have just written and "run" your first computer
program. Congratulations!

Commands with line numbers are known as *program
lines* or *statements*. A group of program lines is called a

program. The computer does not do anything with program lines until you instruct it to "run" the lines.

COMMANDS AND PROGRAMS

The Timex/Sinclair 1000, by itself, is only a box with electronic circuits inside. To get the computer to perform a desired task, you must use its own special language to issue commands that tell the computer what to do. Try this command again:

PRINT "HELLO"

The computer prints the word HELLO on the TV.

You just gave the Timex/Sinclair 1000 a direct command. The word **PRINT** in the command above is an example of a keyword. A keyword tells the computer what kind of action to take; **PRINT** tells the computer to print something. The Timex/Sinclair 1000 has 54 keywords, and at least one must be used every time you give the machine a command.

Before our discussion of commands and programs, it's important to understand how the computer keeps track of your program: *memory.*

Most calculators have some sort of user-accessible memory; when you want to use a number again later, you store it in the calculator's memory. Some expensive calculators have several memory slots, each of which can hold one number.

As you might suspect, computers also have memory to store values for later recall.

Calculators have a fixed number of these memory slots, but you can create as many as you want on the T/S 1000. For example, try this command:

LET NUM = 7

The LET command creates a *cubbyhole* (or a place in memory) called NUM, then places the value 7 in it. Thereafter, the computer substitutes the *value* in the cubbyhole for the *name* of the cubbyhole. You can use a **PRINT** command to find out what is in the cubbyhole NUM:

PRINT NUM

A 7 appears on the TV screen.

You can use a **LET** command either to create or to change the value in NUM:

LET NUM = 117

If you **PRINT** NUM now, the number 117 appears on your TV. Because the value in these cubbyholes may be changed at any time, they are called *variables*. In contrast, numbers that you give to the computer (like the number 117 to the right of the equal sign) are called *constants*. Strings of characters enclosed in quotation marks are called *string constants* or *literals*.

A variable (the cubbyhole) used to hold a number can have any name, as long as it begins with a letter and contains only letters, numbers, and spaces. All of the following names are legal variable names.

    X
    CHERRIES
    AMOUNT
    WB20TM
    GOODBYE APRIL OLD FRIEND

The computer "ignores" spaces, so the last variable name looks the same to the computer as:

    GOODBYEAPRILOLDFRIEND

This is also the same as:

    G O O D B Y E   A P R I L   O L D   F R I E N D

The equal sign (=) in the **LET** statement is used to assign a new value to the variable. This does not have quite the same meaning as the equal sign you are accustomed to using in arithmetic. When used with **LET**, the equals sign means "take the value," or "be equal to the value," so that

LET RASPBERRIES = 14

can be read as "Let the variable RASPBERRIES assume the value 14." In other words, the value 14 is *assigned* to the variable RASPBERRIES. Hence any statement beginning with the keyword **LET** is called an *assignment statement*.

LET commands may also look like this one:

LET NUM = NUM + 10

Enter that command, then **PRINT** NUM. NUM now has the value 127. The computer first finds the value of the "expression" on the right side of the equal sign (in this case, NUM + 10) and then places (assigns) that value into the variable on the left side. The current value of NUM is used to calculate the new value of the expression. NUM + 10 means "Add 10 to the current value of NUM and put the result back in NUM."

Variables can also be used to hold strings, in which case they are called *string variables.* Strings are merely groups of characters. They have no numeric value. You cannot, for example, multiply two strings. String variables are named with one letter followed by a dollar sign ($). Some legal string variables names are:

A$
Z$
I$
P$

Since there are 26 letters in the alphabet, there are 26 available string variables.

Create a string variable by giving it a value, in the same way you create a numerical variable. Try typing this command:

LET A$ = "SOPHOMORES USE LILACS"

Now type this command:

PRINT A$

The computer prints the string.

Now, having memory and variables in mind, we can see how the computer "remembers" commands. When a list of direct commands is given, each command is performed as you type it.

Type the following sequence of commands:

LET A = 10
LET B = 5
LET C = 100
PRINT A + B + C

This command is equivalent to:

PRINT 10 + 5 + 100

However, by using variables, you can write far more efficient, flexible, and useful programs, as you will see later.

You can make up lists of commands, giving each command an identifying number, called a *line number*, and then tell the computer to do everything on the list.

A list of numbered commands is called a program. The commands in a program are called statements. Type this statement:

10 **PRINT** 10 + 5 + 100

When you pressed **ENTER**, the statement disappeared from the bottom line of your TV, then reappeared at the top. You now have a one-line program in your computer's memory. The computer does nothing else with the program until you tell it to execute the commands in the program. Order the computer to execute the program by typing:

RUN

The computer prints 115. You can **RUN** this one-line program as many times as you like, and each time the computer will print 115.

Try typing in this program:

10 **LET** A = 10
20 **LET** B = 5
30 **LET** C = 100
40 **PRINT** A + B + C

Typing a new statement number 10 erases the old one. Now type **RUN**. Once again the computer prints 115 on your TV screen.

Here is what is happening, in detail, in our program. The

computer takes the first value, 10, and stores it in the variable A. It then puts the second value, 5, into the variable B, and the third value, 100, into the variable C. The final line, 40, instructs the computer to add and print A, B, and C. The computer therefore reads the value contained in each variable, then adds them together, and prints the total on your TV screen.

Replace lines 10, 20, and 30 by typing:

```
10 INPUT A
20 INPUT B
30 INPUT C
```

As you **ENTER** the statements, the computer adds them to the program listing at the top of the screen. Statement 40, **PRINT** A + B + C, is still in memory, so you don't have to type it again. Type **RUN** to execute the program.

Nothing appears to happen. The statement **INPUT** A means "Get a value for A from the keyboard." (If, as in this example, the variable A does not exist prior to the **INPUT** statement, the computer creates a variable by that name.)

To continue with this example, enter a 50. The computer takes that, then waits for a value for B. Enter a 20. Now the computer waits for a value for C. Enter a 7. Finally, after the last value has been entered, the computer prints out 77, the sum of A, B, and C.

This is a simple example of why a program is superior to a mere list of commands. This program just adds a short list of numbers together; if the list were long or complex, the computer would save a tremendous amount of time.

When you issue the computer a direct command (a command without a line number), the command is executed immediately, and the command line disappears. Therefore, direct commands are executed in *immediate mode*, also called *command mode*.

When you assign line numbers to commands, the computer saves the lines and does not execute the commands until you tell it to do so. Program lines are executed in *program mode*. With few exceptions, commands may be used either in immediate or program mode. In the program mode, however, you are allowed to stop the program, **RUN** it, edit it, and so on. In general, a computer in the immediate mode is really just a fancy, powerful calculator. Program mode allows the computer to function as a true computer.

You've learned how to install your Timex/Sinclair 1000, how to operate its keyboard, and how to interpret what you see on the screen. You've been introduced to strings, variables, and commands. You now know enough to put your Timex/Sinclair to work. In the next two chapters, you will write your first real, functioning program: a dice game. You'll also learn some new programming features to add to your programming "toolkit."

3

Introductory Concepts

You may have noticed that the bottom of the screen frequently shows two numbers, such as 0/100. Numbers that appear here are known as *report codes* and serve to inform you why the computer has ceased to **RUN** your program. The 0/ means the computer successfully performed what you asked it to, while the 0/100 means that it ran out of program lines after line 100. Type **PRINT** and **ENTER** to erase the HELLO.

The computer may be instructed to execute (or run) the program either with the **RUN** command, or with a **GOTO** command. The G key has **GOTO** printed above it. Now that the K cursor is displayed again, touch the G key. **GOTO** appears on the TV. Type 100. The bottom line of the screen should look like this:

```
GOTO 100
```

This command means "Begin program execution at line 100."

Press **ENTER**.

The word HELLO appears again. Using **RUN** or **GOTO**, a program may be run as many times as you like. **RUN** and **GOTO**, however, are slightly different. The differences will become clear later. For now, type the following line:

```
200 GOTO 100
```

Press **ENTER**. This line and the line 100 that you previously typed appear at the top of the screen. New numbered lines are automatically added in numerical order to the computer's internal program list. Whenever you choose, you may begin executing this list: type **RUN** and press **ENTER**.

The left side of the screen fills with HELLOs.

When the computer executes the command in line 100, HELLO is printed on the screen. The computer then executes line 200, which tells it to jump back and repeat line 100. This continues until the screen is full. The bottom line of the screen displays 5/100. The 5 is the report code, which means that the screen is full. The 100 means the computer was trying to execute line 100 at the time the screen became full. Remember, whenever you see a report code, it is a signal that your program has stopped executing, usually because of an error. The T/S 1000 has a total of 15 report codes; these are listed in Appendix F at the end of this book.

The C key is labeled **CONT**, for **CONTINUE**. Touch the C key, and the word **CONT** appears at the bottom of the screen. Press **ENTER**. Another screen full of HELLOs appears, and the message 5/100 appears on the bottom again. Type **CONT** and **ENTER** again. The screen fills once more. You could continue this indefinitely. The two-line program

```
100 PRINT "HELLO"
200 GOTO 100
```

will loop around forever. This kind of loop is referred to as an *infinite loop* because it will never end by itself. True, this infinite loop stops when the screen fills, but only because the screen cannot contain any more lines, not because the loop has been "broken." To terminate a loop without turning the computer off, use the **BREAK** keyword located on the **SPACE** key. The **BREAK** is your way to interrupt a program while it's running.

To view your program, type the keyword **LIST**. Since **LIST** is located above the K key, touch K to make the word **LIST** appear. Type **ENTER**. The computer prints its numbered list of commands—the program consisting of the two lines printed at the top of the screen. **LIST** prints the computer's program list on the screen.

Type the following line:

50 **PRINT** "A SCREEN OF HELLOS"

Press **ENTER**.

The line 50 appears above the lines 100 and 200.

When a program line is entered, the computer always puts it in numerical order. This is a significant feature because programs are executed in sequence from the smallest line number to the largest (except where you insert **GOTO** statements to change the logical "flow" of the program).

Notice that there is a small arrow inside a black box between the 50 and the **PRINT**. That arrow points to the *current line* of the program. Look at the 5, 6, 7, and 8 keys. Each of them has an arrow printed on it. You have already used the right- and left-pointing arrows to move a line on the bottom of the screen. The up and down arrows, however, are used to move the *current line pointer*. Hold **SHIFT** and press the 6 key. The current line pointer moves down to line 100.

The red word on the 1 key in the upper left corner of the keyboard is **EDIT**. When you edit a sentence on a piece of paper, you use a pencil and an eraser to make corrections. Similarly, the computer has commands to insert or remove portions of a program line. Making changes in your program is called *editing*. Hold **SHIFT** and press **EDIT**.

The line 100, **PRINT** "HELLO", is copied to the bottom of the screen. You can now make changes in this copy. Use the right-pointing arrow (→) (**SHIFT**/8) to move the cursor to the right end of the line. Add a semicolon (;) to the line by holding **SHIFT** and pressing the X key. The line now looks like this:

100 **PRINT** "HELLO";

Press **ENTER**, and the new version of line 100 replaces the original one up above. Now type **RUN** and press **ENTER**. The screen fills with HELLOs from edge to edge.

The semicolon at the end of the **PRINT** line means "Don't start another line—continue printing at the current location." Notice that at the end of each line, HELLO is split. When a line is full, the computer automatically drops down and begins writing at the beginning of the next line. A line holds 32 characters: 22 lines fit on the screen, plus a 23rd and 24th line on the bottom for report codes and a "command" line.

Type the following line. (Do not put quotation marks around the 5.)

PRINT 5

Press **ENTER**. A 5 appears in the upper left corner of the screen. Numbers do not have to be in quotation marks when you print them. In fact, the computer treats them differently (that is, like any other string) when they are in quotation marks. Try typing the following two lines, pressing **ENTER** after each one. (From now on, you won't always be reminded that you have to press **ENTER** after each line; but if you don't, the computer won't do anything.) Think of **ENTER** as the period at the end of your command.

PRINT "1+3+4+5"
PRINT 1+3+4+5

The first time, the computer just printed the *string* 1+3+4+5 on the TV screen. The second time, the computer printed the number 13 on the TV, since 13 is the sum of the numbers. When you give a string to the computer, it treats the string as a single unit. When you give a number to the computer, it uses the value of that number. So, when you gave the line **PRINT** 1+3+4+5, the computer added the numbers together.

Type **PRINT** and a quotation mark again (**PRINT** "). (Don't forget to press **ENTER**.)

The line stays on the bottom of the screen. Notice that next to the cursor is a black box with a white S in it. That indicates that the computer could not accept the line because the wording or spelling was wrong. Just as you may have trouble understanding a grammatically incorrect sentence, the computer cannot understand incorrect commands. It understands only a strictly limited vocabulary. If you misspell a word or enter a command (or group of commands) incorrectly, the computer won't know what you want it to do. It will reject the line and put an S before the part that it doesn't understand.

In our example above, the computer is confused because you gave it only one quotation mark. Quotation marks *must* come in pairs. Errors of this type are indicated by the S (which stands for *syntax*).

As a matter of brevity, we will now use the term **SHIFT/**

keyname to mean "Press **SHIFT** and the named key." For example, **SHIFT**/A means "Simultaneously depress the **SHIFT** key and the letter A."

EXPRESSIONS

The examples you have seen so far have included some mathematical operations. Specifically, you have seen this line:

    PRINT 1+3+4+5

A group of numbers connected by plus signs (+) or other operators is called a *numerical expression*. You are probably familiar with ordinary mathematical operations: addition, subtraction, multiplication, and division. Whenever you use one of those operations, you are creating a numerical expression. The Timex/Sinclair 1000 contains an *expression handler*, which is used every time an expression is found in a command. The expression handler calculates the final value of the expression. Since the expression handler is called whenever an expression is found, you may use an expression almost anywhere you use a numerical value. The only exception is in numbering program lines. The following command will not be accepted:

    5+100 **PRINT** "HELLO"

You can, however, use expressions in other places where a line number is needed. You may use a **GOTO** statement like this one:

    200 **GOTO** 100+BASE

The expression handler will first find the value contained in the variable BASE, then add 100 to it, after which the program jumps to the line number with the resulting value. Of course, the variable BASE must already have been created before the program can execute line 200.

The operators you can use in expressions are:

        addition   +
      subtraction   −

multiplication	*
division	/
exponentiation	**

These operators appear in red on the K, J, B, V, and H keys. Type them by holding **SHIFT** and pressing the appropriate key.

Addition (+) and subtraction (−) work in the usual way.

Multiplication uses as its symbol an asterisk (*), to avoid confusion with the more customary multiplication symbols (×, ·) with the letter X and the period.

In division (/) the first number entered is divided by the second. Try this example:

PRINT 10/2

The computer divides 10 by 2 and prints the answer, 5.

Ordinary fractions are usually written in decimal form. For example, $10\frac{1}{2}$ is written 10.5. You could write $10 + 1/2$, but the decimal form is simpler.

Our final operator, exponentiation, may not be familiar. Exponentiation is also referred to as "raising a number to a power." It is usually written with the power as a superscript and with the power digit one-half line above the base number. For example, 2 raised to the 5th power is written as 2^5. This means that 2 is multiplied by itself five times ($2*2*2*2*2$), and the result is 32. Here is an example that shows the power of exponentiation.

There were about 100 Pilgrims on the *Mayflower*. Normal population growth is about 2% a year, which results in the population of *Mayflower* descendants doubling every 35 years. That means that the original population of 100 or so Pilgrims has doubled about 10.3 times in the last 360 years.

If you type in this statement, you will see how many *Mayflower* descendants there may be in the United States. Typing two single asterisks (*) together will not work. You must use the double asterisk (**) on the H key (**SHIFT**/H).

PRINT 100*2**10.3

The five valid operators that may be used in numerical expressions are not necessarily executed from left to right. Try typing in this command:

PRINT 5 − 4*3

The computer prints −7 (negative seven). Had the expression evaluator simply gone through the expression from left to right, it would have first subtracted 4 from 5, leaving 1, then multiplied 1 by 3, resulting in 3. In fact, the expression evaluator performs the 4*3 operation first and then subtracts the result, 12, from 5.

The expression evaluator first performs functions, then exponentiations. Next it performs multiplication and division, followed by addition and subtraction.

If there are more than one multiplication or division, these are done left to right. If there are more than one addition or subtraction, they, too, are performed left to right.

Anything enclosed in parentheses is evaluated first, using the priorities already mentioned. Parentheses may be used at any time to make your expressions easier to visualize and understand. Anything preceded by a minus sign (which looks just like a subtraction sign but indicates a number that is less than zero) is evaluated immediately after exponentiation.

To summarize, the order of priorities is:

1. contents of parentheses
2. functions
3. exponentiation (**)
4. negative numbers (−)
5. multiplication and division (*, /)
6. addition and subtraction (+, −)

Strings, however, have only one operator, +. The + operator adds two strings together. Try this command:

PRINT "CAT" + "MOUSE"

The computer prints CATMOUSE. Any spaces outside the quotation marks are ignored.

String variables may be used as string expressions. Type these commands:

LET A$ = "MULE" + "DEER"
LET B$ = "HORSE"
PRINT A$ + B$ + "FISH"

The computer prints MULEDEERHORSEFISH on the TV screen.

A string expression may always be used in place of a constant string.

There are four commands that affect all variables on the computer: **CLEAR, NEW, RUN,** and **LOAD**.

CLEAR destroys all variables.

RUN destroys all variables and then runs any program loaded in the computer.

NEW wipes everything from memory: all variables and all program statements are forever lost.

The **LOAD** command destroys all variables and programs when it loads new ones from a tape. Variables stored on tape are preserved.

All four commands clear the screen. You may clear the screen without changing variables or program statements by using the **CLS** (clear screen) command.

As your programming abilities increase, you will discover that your programs become more complicated. As this occurs, you will find it progressively more difficult to remember what specific lines in your program are intended to do. Programs that you labored over for hours will look totally unfamiliar to you in a few weeks, and you will be forced to try to reconstruct the thinking that led you to write the lines. It is frequently more difficult to rediscover a thought than to have it in the first place! Wouldn't it be nice if we could leave notes to ourselves explaining what we intended, so that at a later date we (or someone else) would have insight into our programming genius?

Luckily, BASIC provides just such a feature: the **REM** (**REMARK**) statement. Whenever your computer encounters a line such as

100 REM A$ = THE NAME OF THE PLAYER

it will simply ignore everything following the **REM**. No report code will be generated because the **REM** signals that the program is to jump to the next line.

The next time you want to look at your program, you will find your reminder that A$ = THE NAME OF THE PLAYER and will not have to figure it out from the context of the program.

Unfortunately, memory space is so precious on the basic

Timex/Sinclair 1000 that we have chosen not to include **REM** statements in the programs presented in this book. But the generous use of **REM** statements is generally considered to be as essential to good programming practice as, say, logical thought. If you elect in the future to purchase the 16K memory extension, we heartily recommend that you begin immediately to leave yourself these important notes.

4

A Program for Playing Dice

A very common simple program is a dice game. This is of limited use—your home computer will never be as portable, or as quickly available, as a pair of dice. On the other hand, a dice program has the advantage of using a number of the more common types of programming statements; therefore, once you understand how a dice program works, you will be able to write your own simple programs.

When approaching a programming problem, your first step should be to lay out exactly what you want the program to do.

You could make up your own list, but this one was used to design the program described in this chapter.

1. Find out how many dice are required by player.
2. Give player opportunity to terminate game.
3. Pick a die side.
4. **GOTO** (2) the required number of times.

Here is the entire program. Type it in now, and run it to get a feel for the way it works. Later in this chapter, the program is examined in detail. Remember that the boldface words are keywords, which must be entered with a single keystroke. **INPUT, IF, CLS, FOR, PRINT, NEXT,** and **GOTO** (the first keywords on each program line) will print when you touch the letter key above which the keyword is written. You get the keywords **THEN, STOP,** and **TO,** which are written in red, by holding **SHIFT** and pressing the key on which each is written. The **INT** and **RND** keywords are a new type, "function" keywords, that will be explained later. For the moment, when it is time to type **INT**, hold **SHIFT** and press **ENTER** (labeled FUNCTION in red). The cursor will change from █ to ▐. Then press the key with **INT** written *under* it, and the **INT** keyword appears. The ▐ cursor also changes back to an █. To type **RND**, do the same thing: type **SHIFT-ENTER**, then touch the R key, which has **RND** written below it.

```
50 PRINT "HOW MANY DICE TO ROLL?"
100 INPUT A
200 CLS
300 IF A=0 THEN STOP
500 PRINT INT (1+6*RND)
600 LET A=A−1
700 GOTO 300
```

Now run the program. Type:

RUN

Don't forget to press **ENTER**. When you are finished playing with the program, terminate it by entering 0 for the number of dice to roll.

Step 1—which was to find out how many dice are required by the player—was easy to put into the program. You've seen **INPUT** statements before, and one is needed here.

100 INPUT A

Statement 200 contains the **CLS** (clear screen) command. After you **ENTER** the number of dice to be displayed, the program erases everything on the screen to leave a blank field for the new dice. You also need a way to terminate the program. If the person using the dice program asks for 0 dice, the program detects the 0 and ends. A statement is needed that says, "If A is equal to 0, stop the program." This is done with the statement:

300 IF A=0 THEN STOP

This is an example of an **IF . . . THEN** statement.

IF . . . THEN statements allow a computer to make decisions. In general, an **IF . . . THEN** statement has this form:

(line number) **IF** (condition is true) **THEN** (command)

You may have noticed that the █ cursor appears after you type the keyword **THEN**. The command following the **THEN** can be any legal BASIC command. In the case of statement 300, the command is **STOP**, which means "Stop the program."

The **IF** is known as a *relational expression*. Every relational expression is either true or false. For example, statement 300 has the relational expression **IF** A=0. If A does, in fact, equal 0, the command that comes after **THEN** is executed. If A is not equal to 0, then the **STOP** is not executed and the program jumps immediately to the next line.

The relationship used in this particular relational expression is "equals," but equality is not the only valid relational expression. There are six ways in which two values can be related. The first value can be

1. greater than (>),
2. less than (<),
3. equal to (=),
4. less than or equal to (< =),
5. greater than or equal to (> =)
6. not equal to (< >)

the second value.

In each case, if the relational expression is true, the command after the **THEN** is executed. If the relationship is false, the command immediately following the **THEN** is ignored, and the program continues execution at the next line number.

Here are some commands you can try using **IF . . . THEN**. (Typing in commands without line numbers will not affect the program statements you've already typed in.)

```
LET DOG = 7
LET CAT = 8
IF DOG < CAT THEN PRINT "CATS ARE BEST"
```

The message is printed on your screen since the value of DOG, 7, is less than the value of CAT, 8.

The command after the **THEN** can be another **IF . . . THEN** statement. Try this:

IF DOG < > CAT **THEN IF** CAT = 8 **THEN IF** DOG = 7 **THEN PRINT** "CATS ARE EIGHT"

Since each relational expression in each of the three **IF . . . THEN** statements is true, the message prints.

There is an easier way to write very long compound **IF** statements. You can connect relational expressions with the two keywords **AND** and **OR**. (Type these keywords by pressing **SHIFT** and 2 for **AND**, and **SHIFT/W** for **OR**.) Each of these can be used to connect two relational expressions.

Try typing this statement:

IF DOG < > CAT **AND** CAT = 8 **AND** DOG = 7 **THEN PRINT** "CATS ARE STILL EIGHT"

This statement has exactly the same effect as the compound **IF** statement you typed in before, but it is more efficient (it saves memory and execution time), because the computer has fewer keywords to interpret and act upon.

When two relational expressions are connected with **AND**, the two together are true only if each of them is individually true. The **IF** statement above may be translated as: If DOG is not equal to CAT, and if CAT equals 8 and DOG equals 7, then print "CATS ARE STILL EIGHT."

When two relational expressions are connected with **OR**, the two together are true if either of the two is true. Try this statement:

IF DOG > CAT **OR** DOG < CAT **THEN PRINT** "DOGS ARE DIFFERENT"

The message is printed because, even though the first relational expression (DOG > CAT) is false, the second (DOG < CAT) is true.

You may use **AND** and **OR** to chain together as many relational expressions as you like.

Back to the dice program. Step 2 of the plan for this program was to pick a die side. The program itself must pick a number to represent the number of dots on one side of a die.

When a die is rolled, it comes to rest with one of its sides up; which side is up is purely a matter of chance. In computer terms, the die can be said to have "picked" a random number between 1 and 6. *Random* indicates that one number is as likely to come up as any other, every time you roll. Suppose the die comes up a 6. If you pick up the die and roll it again, there is a one-in-six chance that you will get a 6, 3, 1, 2, 4, or 5. Each time you roll the die, there is an equal chance that any one of the sides will come up.

The T/S 1000 has the ability to generate random numbers through the use of the **RND** function.

Functions are special programs, permanently stored inside the computer. Each function produces some number or letter. Functions can be used in place of a constant, or in an expression. Functions are treated in more depth in the next chapter, but for now just regard them as prepackaged programs that are part of the BASIC toolkit.

Functions are always indicated by keywords. To type a function keyword, first hold the **SHIFT** and press **ENTER** at the same time. On the **ENTER** key, you will see the word FUNCTION in red. By pressing **SHIFT/ENTER**, you are invoking the function facility. Notice that nothing was printed, but the cursor has now changed to an **F** cursor. This indicates that the computer expects your next entry to be a function. Notice that many of the keys have labels below them. For example, Q, W, and E have **SIN**, **COS**, and **TAN** below them. Those are function keywords, and, when the **F** cursor is displayed and you touch one of these keys, the function keyword is displayed. (Actually, not all of the words below the keys are functions. Some serve other purposes but are written below the keys for convenience. In any case, you can type only the keywords below the keys when the **F** cursor is displayed.) **RND** appears below the T key, so, to use the **RND** function, press **SHIFT** and **ENTER**, then release both keys and press T. The **F** cursor stays on for only one keystroke, after which it is replaced immediately by the **L** cursor.

RND is a simple function to use. Try typing this command:

PRINT RND

The computer prints a long number between 0 and 1. Try **PRINT RND** again several more times; you should get a different number each time. The numbers being generated are not truly random, but are "pseudorandom." The sequence of these numbers has been programmed to provide the appearance of randomness, so that when you enter a program that requires random number generation (such as our dice program), the **RND** function can effectively satisfy that requirement. From now on, when we refer to a random number generated by the computer, you will know that we are really talking about pseudorandom numbers.

The computer always produces a random number between 0 and 1; but a die always produces a random number between 1 and 6. Try typing the following command:

PRINT 1+6*RND

This command will always produce a number between 1 and 6. It is not exactly like your die, however, because a die always produces a *whole* number, or *integer*. That is, a die will always give a 1, 2, 3, 4, 5, or 6, but never, for example, a 1.5. The first time you type **PRINT** 1+6*RND, the computer might give you, say, 5.7415161. The second time it might give you 2.6150818.

To make the computer act like a die, we need to crop off everything to the right of the decimal point. The **INT** function of the T/S 1000 does just that: it converts a number into an integer by dropping everything to the right of the decimal point. Try typing the following command. (Remember that in order to get **INT**, you must press **SHIFT/ENTER** so that the **F** cursor appears, then press the R key. Since the **F** cursor only stays on for one keystroke, you will have to get it back again to type **RND**.)

PRINT INT (1+6*RND)

The computer prints a whole number between 1 and 6.

The parentheses in the statement cause **INT** to return the integer for the entire expression inside the parentheses. Functions generally operate only on the digit immediately following the function keyword. Without the parentheses, **INT** would return the integer of 1, which wouldn't be of much help.

As you can see, functions can be useful short cuts in

writing programs. There are 21 functions on the Timex/Sinclair 1000; the most important ones are used in programs in Chapters 8 through 11. Check the manual that came with your computer for descriptions of the rest when you need them.

The final form for our random whole-number statement is:

500 **PRINT INT** (1+6*RND)

That completes steps 1 and 2 of the plan for this program. Step 3 is to go back to (2) for the required number of times.

Statement 100, **INPUT A**, gets the number of dice from the player. The program must then execute statement 500 the correct number of times (that is, the number of times equal to the value of A).

Here's the program again to refresh your memory:

```
50 PRINT "HOW MANY DICE TO ROLL?"
100 INPUT A
200 CLS
300 IF A=0 THEN STOP
500 PRINT INT (1+6*RND)
600 LET A=A-1
700 GOTO 300
```

By writing the program using **LET** A=A−1 and **GOTO** 300, every time a number is printed, 1 will be subtracted from A. When A is equal to 0, the conditional clause in the **IF** statement on line 300 will be true and the program will stop.

This completes our initial plan for the dice program. You've come a long way and learned a lot of new concepts. If anything is not clear to you at this point, review it until you feel comfortable with it; then read the next chapter on how to save your dice program on cassette tape for later use.

We're not finished with the dice program, however; in Chapter 7 we'll add some new "bells and whistles" to make the dice themselves actually show up on the screen! If your're really anxious to get on with more programming, jump right into Chapter 6.

5

Saving Programs on Tape

Unlike most people, computers are not at all bothered by the monotony of repetition. If it were necessary to type in a program every time you wanted to balance your checkbook, play a game, or just work on the program, you might quickly become bored and frustrated. With the aid of an ordinary tape recorder, your computer can relieve you of that tedium.

SAVING PROGRAMS ON CASSETTE

When you have worked hard typing a program, it's a shame to have all your work disappear when the T/S 1000 is turned off. Fortunately, if you own an inexpensive tape recorder, you can easily store your programs on cassette tapes. You can also load programs from other cassettes into your computer. For the next few paragraphs, we'll discuss the types of tape recorders and tapes that will yield the best results.

THE CASSETTE RECORDER

The most suitable kind of cassette recorder is an inexpensive monaural (*not* stereo) recorder. A tape deck that is part of a large stereo system is definitely not recommended.

The recorder must have external microphone (MIC) and

earphone (EAR) jacks. Included with your Timex computer was a short double cord with two plugs on each end; those fit into the tape recorder's MIC and EAR sockets. (Inexpensive recorders are more likely to have the appropriate jacks.) If your tape recorder is equipped with a single earphone, there is a good chance it is compatible with the computer.

A program counter on the recorder can be very useful. This device counts as the tape goes by. You can use the numbers thus displayed to locate programs on long tapes. Counters are not usually very accurate, though, so you should use the counter only to determine the approximate location of a program.

THE CASSETTE

You can use almost any brand of cassette, although you should avoid very inexpensive ones if you value the programs you are putting on them. Cassettes intended for computers (C-10 or C-12) work best.

Get the shortest cassettes possible. Compared with your T/S 1000's memory, a cassette holds a lot of information. Since the entire memory of your computer takes less than a minute to be written onto a cassette, your programs will be easier to find if there is only one program per cassette side.

Very short (5 minutes on a side) cassettes are available from computer dealers and electronics stores.

You will have less trouble if you use new cassettes. Many recorders do not erase tape very well, and the noise left over from previous recordings can cause problems.

As a safeguard in the event a tape is damaged or accidentally erased, it's a good idea to make backup copies of important programs. One of the following sections contains a discussion on copying tapes. Once you have your program on tape, take good care of the cassette. Keep it away from magnetic fields, permanent magnets, and your TV.

"CANNED" PROGRAMS

The predecessors of the Timex/Sinclair 1000, the Sinclair ZX80 and ZX81, have been the largest-selling computers in the world. Consequently, a vast library of programs has been developed for use on the T/S 1000. There are accounting, educational, graphics, and of course game programs available for your computer.

Sinclair user groups currently exist across the United States and around the world. Once the Timex computer has been on the market for a while, there may be user groups in almost every city. These groups are clubs that exist to share information about computers. In addition to exchanging tips, programming hints, and other bits of knowledge, members are encouraged to share programs. Many commercial organizations (including Timex and Sinclair) sell programs; in any case, prerecorded cassettes are widely available.

Several magazines exist solely for the users of the Timex and Sinclair computers. (The addresses of some of these magazines are given in Appendix C at the back of this book.) These magazines often review commercial programs. Unfortunately, since there are so many programs and so few magazines, much of the good software goes unreviewed.

Whether you purchase programs or get them from a personal source, be certain that the programs have been written for either the Timex/Sinclair 1000 or the Sinclair ZX81. Each computer has its own idiosyncrasies, so programs written for other computers will not run on the T/S 1000. The fact that a program has been written in BASIC does not necessarily mean it will work on the T/S 1000—every company's BASIC is unique. Even programs written for the Sinclair ZX80 (the earlier model of the Sinclair ZX81) may not work on your Timex/Sinclair.

A program's memory requirement is an important consideration in buying software. Your Timex/Sinclair 1000 is supplied with a little more than 2,000 bytes of user memory. A *byte* is a single piece of information (such as the letter A). In computer terms, 2,000 bytes of user memory are called 2K of RAM (random access memory). The Sinclair ZX81 comes with 1K of RAM, or only half as much user memory as the T/S 1000. Therefore, programs written for an ordinary Sinclair ZX81 will fit into your Timex computer. However, many programs are written especially for the ZX81 or Timex/Sinclair with extra memory. The most common memory extension increases the memory to 16K; this means that larger programs can be used on the computer. Programs written for 16K of memory will not fit into your Timex computer without a memory extension. (See Appendix A for more information.) If you buy program cassettes at a store or by mail, the package or ad should stipulate the amount of memory required. If an advertisement isn't clear and if you don't own a memory extension, be wary about buying the program. If you are receiving the software from a friend or a user group, you may save time if you find out in advance whether the program will fit into your computer.

Once you have the cassette with the program, loading it into your computer is like loading any other program from cassette. See the section "Loading Programs from Tape" later in this chapter for instructions on the procedure.

You should always make a copy of any program that you buy, then store the original cassette away from electronic equipment or magnetic fields. See the section "Copying a Tape" later in this chapter.

HOW TO SAVE PROGRAMS

Type a program into the computer. (Use a short program for practice; for example, try the calculator program in Chapter 11.) Once loaded, **LIST** the program to make certain that it is actually there. Now, set the tape to the beginning. Put your recorder on RECORD. Next, using the microphone, record the name of the program; then turn off the recorder. By recording the program's name onto the tape, you'll be able to find the program later on.

A short cord with two plugs on each end was supplied with your computer. The four plugs are of two different colors. Plug any end into the MIC socket on your recorder, and the other end *with the same color* into the MIC socket of the computer. These sockets are next to the power plug. Do *not* plug the other part of the cord into the EAR sockets yet.

Set your recorder's volume about three-quarters of the way up. If your recorder has automatic volume control, don't worry about the volume. If the recorder has a single tone control, turn it all the way up. If the recorder has bass and treble controls, turn the bass all the way down and the treble all the way up.

Now you are ready to store your program on tape.

Type the following command into the computer (but don't press **ENTER** yet):

SAVE "program name"

The **SAVE** keyword is generated by touching the S key when the ◼ cursor is displayed. Use any program name you choose, but select one that is related to the program's purpose. For example if you are using the *Better Calculator* from Chapter 11, use "Calculator" as the program name. The name can be as long as you like (up to 127 characters) and can contain spaces. Do not use inverse video characters in the name.

Now set your recorder to RECORD; if you are starting at the beginning of the tape, let it run for 5 seconds before you type **ENTER**. This delay will allow the blank tape at the end (called the leader) to pass by. Then press **ENTER**. The TV screen will go blank for a few seconds, then it will be covered with rapidly shifting, thin lines. After a few seconds, the screen will go blank again and the report code 0/0 will appear in the lower left corner, indicating that all went well. Turn your recorder off. Type this command (but don't press **ENTER** yet):

SAVE "program name"

Use the same program name. Turn your recorder on again and press **ENTER**. When the 0/0 appears, go through the same process a third time. It's a good idea to make two or three copies. Occasionally, through an accident or a defect on the tape, one or two of the copies may become damaged. The computer will not be able to load an even partially damaged tape, so making three copies will provide some insurance.

Cassettes have tabs on the back of the housings near the corners. If these are removed, nothing can be recorded on that cassette. This is a form of permanent protection for your programs against accidental erasure by your recorder. If you later decide to record over the tape, simply put tape over the holes where the tabs once were.

LOADING PROGRAMS FROM TAPE

Rewind the tape, unplug the cord from the MIC socket, then plug the cord into the EAR (or MONITOR) socket of the recorder; and the other plug of the same color into the EAR socket of your computer. You should not have the cord plugged into both the EAR and MIC sockets at the same time. Many tape recorders will not work correctly with the computer if both the EAR and the MIC sockets are connected.

Type the following command (but don't press **ENTER** yet):

   LOAD "program name"

The program name you give must be exactly the same as the one you used when you saved the program. If the original name contained spaces, this one must have spaces also.

Now set the volume control on the recorder about three-quarters of the way up and press **ENTER**.

The screen will show diagonal lines for a few seconds, then thick horizontal bands will appear for a few seconds. The horizontal bands are caused by the recorded version of the program.

When the horizontal bands disappear, the TV screen should go blank except for a 0/0 in the lower left corner. If the diagonal lines return, the computer was unable to load the tape copy of the program. Let the tape continue, to see if the second or third copies work.

If none of the three copies works, or if the horizontal bands never appear, press the **BREAK** key (the **SPACE** key) to prevent the computer from waiting needlessly for the tape.

If the 0/0 appeared, everything went fine. Now press **LIST** to see that the program is, in fact, the one you wanted. If so, then skip the rest of this section.

If, however, the computer did not successfully get the program off the tape, there are a few things you can do. Here are the possible problems and some solutions:

• The volume may not be high enough. Try turning it up. If that doesn't work, the volume may be too high, and you should try turning it down. (It is, however, unlikely that the volume is too high.)
• Check the tone controls (if there are any) to see if the treble is turned all the way up and the bass all the way down. If there is only one tone control, turn it all the way up.
• The plugs may not be secure, or they may be in the wrong sockets. To get a program from the tape, the cord should be in the EAR socket of both the tape recorder and the computer. The same color plug should be plugged into each. Make certain that the plugs are in as far as possible. If the

plug is loose or too tight, your tape recorder's EAR socket may require a different-sized plug. Adaptors are available at electronics stores.

• The recorder may be stereophonic. Monophonic ones work more reliably for saving and loading tapes.

• You may have used all four plugs during recording. This can record interference on the tape. Try rerecording.

• If you are using a prerecorded program cassette, it may be intended for another computer. The tape must be for the Timex/Sinclair 1000 or the Sinclair ZX81. You cannot use tapes made for another company's computer.

• If you are using a prerecorded program cassette, it may be intended for a T/S 1000 with the memory extension attached. Unless you have a memory extension, you can use only programs intended for an unextended Timex/Sinclair 1000 or Sinclair ZX81. The program's literature should specify how much memory is needed. If you don't have a memory extension, your computer can accept only 1K or 2K programs.

• The tape may have been incorrectly recorded. Some problems can be detected by listening to the tape. Unplug the cord from the recorder and rewind the tape. Turn down the volume, and play the tape. You should hear your voice announcing the name of the program (if you recorded this tape), then a soft buzz. Next should be five seconds of silence. The silence tells the computer to expect a program. The tape recorder may be generating too much noise, or the tape itself may have too much surface noise. You can try loading the program with the volume turned down a bit. After the silence comes a few seconds of a loud, very annoying high-pitched tone. This is the program, after which the soft buzz should return. If you do not get this sequence of sounds, the program probably was not recorded. Carefully record the program again. If that doesn't work, the jacks on the computer or the recorder may be defective. Try another recorder. If you can't get any recorder to work, there's a good chance something is wrong with the computer or the cord. Examine the cord for breaks.

If you purchase a program on cassette but you don't hear the proper sequence of sounds when you listen to it, return it and ask for another copy.

• If you are near a ham radio or commercial radio broadcasting antenna, that may be creating interference. Try moving to another part of the house.

• Some tape recorders pick up hum from the power line. Try running your recorder on batteries, if possible.
• The tape may have noise on it that your recorder cannot erase. Try using a new cassette.
• The tabs may have been removed from your cassette, making it impossible to record. If so, put tape over the holes where the tabs were.
• You may not have run 5 seconds of leader from the beginning of the cassette. Rerecord the program, taking care to let the leader pass before engaging the record lever.

COPYING A TAPE

It is very easy to copy a program from one cassette to another. First load the program into the computer. (See the preceding section for how to do that.) Then put a new cassette into the recorder, and save the program onto the new cassette. You cannot copy an entire cassette at a time; you can only copy one program at a time.

Since it is possible that a piece of the tape's surface may not work well, it is a good idea to make several copies of the program on the new cassette.

PROGRAMS THAT RUN THEMSELVES

The **RUN** command clears all the variables from memory before starting the program. This may be an undesirable action. For example, if a program is designed to keep records, or contains data that is not actually written as part of the program (but rather stored in variables), you can run it by typing **GOTO** 0 (or some other line number). This runs the program without affecting the variables.

Alternatively, you can make the program save itself— variables and all—onto tape. The ability to save values contained in the variables is a powerful feature of your T/S 1000.

Here's how to do it: **SAVE** may be used in a program line. When that line is executed, the program saves itself on tape. (You must, of course have connected the cables, set up the tape recorder, and started the recorder running.) You could use statements like the following:

```
100 SAVE "PROGRAM"
200 GOTO 0
```

The **SAVE** statement will execute, then the **GOTO** statement will execute, and the program will continue running. A program saved on tape in this manner will always begin execution immediately after the **SAVE** statement. When you load the program from the tape, the **GOTO** statement will execute immediately, and the program will start over again. The statement after the **SAVE** does not have to be **GOTO** 0. It can be any legal program statement.

BUILDING FANCY TAPES

If you want to get fancy, you can create programs that automate the process of loading programs. For example, you could write a small program like this one:

```
100 PRINT "ENTER A PROGRAM NAME"
200 PRINT "1    DICE"
300 PRINT "2    CHECK"
400 PRINT "3    RECIPE"
500 PRINT "4    RECORDS"
600 INPUT A
700 GOTO A*1000
1000 LOAD "DICE"
2000 LOAD "CHECK"
3000 LOAD "RECIPE"
4000 LOAD "RECORDS"
```

This "menu" program could be the first one on a tape that also contains DICE, CHECK, RECIPE, and RECORDS. You would load the menu (with a command like **LOAD** "MENU"), run it, then start the recorder playing again, and enter the number for the program you want. The computer would go through the tape until it found the program you specified.

By using the "Programs That Run Themselves" technique (see the previous section) and endless loop cassettes, which you can buy in some computer stores, you can create a tape that would be fully automated. You leave the tape running, and first type **LOAD** "MENU." When the menu loads, it begins running and waits for you to make a selection. Each program on the tape terminates with the statement "Load Menu," which starts the whole cycle again. Unless you use an endless loop tape, you would have to stop, start, and rewind the recorder at the appropriate times.

Unfortunately, there is no easy way for a program to pass data to another program.

6
Powerful Programming Tips

This chapter consists of small programs that do nothing really useful, but each illustrates an important point about BASIC programming. Many topics touched only briefly in previous chapters are covered in greater detail here, and many new topics are introduced as well. Everything in this chapter will be invaluable if you intend to follow along with the explanations in the four programming chapters that follow. Consider the ideas in this chapter as "embellishments" you will need to sharpen your programming skills.

FAST AND SLOW MODES

The T/S 1000 can run at two speeds: **FAST** and **SLOW**. Whenever you turn the computer on, it is in **SLOW** mode. In **SLOW** mode, the TV screen is constantly updated: new information that a program writes to the screen appears immediately. In **FAST** mode, the screen is neglected unless the computer has nothing else to do.

Programs that do a lot of calculating but not much displaying will run about four times faster in **FAST** mode than in **SLOW** mode. On the negative side, hitting a key in

FAST will cause the screen to flicker. Moreover, screen information will be displayed only while the program is waiting for imput or while a **PAUSE** is in effect.

The mode you select is generally just a matter of taste. When the program requires one or the other mode, we'll point it out.

One point, though: if you are entering or examining a program that has more than a few statements in it, you may soon find that you want to work in **FAST** mode. In **FAST** mode, the screen display is constructed first and is then displayed all at once. In **SLOW** mode, the screen is displayed as it builds into a complete image. The waiting can be annoying to some people, so use whichever mode you prefer.

EVERYTHING ABOUT PRINT

By this time, the **PRINT** statement should be familiar to you. This section discusses the ways you can use items in **PRINT** statements to control the way the screen looks.

You have already seen how commas and semicolons change the way the output appears. To sum up, when a print item is followed by a semicolon, the next item printed appears on the same line as, and immediately following, the first item.

Try typing and running this program:

```
10 FOR X=1 TO 10
20 PRINT "A";
30 NEXT X
```

The A's all appear side by side on a single line. Try changing the semicolon to a comma. Run it again. This time the A's appear in two columns. When an item is followed by a comma, the next printed item appears on the other half of the screen. **TAB** and **AT** can be used to change the position where **PRINT** displays your output.

These two items are very similar. **TAB** specifies a column on the current line. **AT** specifies a row and column of the screen.

In both cases, the column is counted from the left and is an absolute position. For example, **TAB** 31 always refers to the rightmost column of the screen.

When followed by a semicolon, **TAB** and **AT** display the next **PRINT** item in the position immediately after the one specified by the **TAB** or **AT**.

Printing normally proceeds from line to line as the lines fill. The *print position* is the position where the next item will be printed. Normally, the **PRINT** position moves down the screen as items are printed. **TAB** doesn't change the direction of the print position as it progresses across and down the screen—it can only move the print position ahead. If the print position is at column 15, and you give the command **PRINT TAB** 5, the print position moves to column 5 of the next line. **PRINT AT**, however, can move the print position to anywhere on the screen. (**PLOT** and **UNPLOT** also can move the print position to anywhere on the screen.)

The commands **CLS, CLEAR, NEW, CONT,** and **RUN** move the print position back to the top left corner of the screen. Also, when any program or direct command finishes execution, the print position is set back to the top left corner.

Try typing in this sample program.

```
100 FOR X=20 TO 1 STEP −2
110 LET Z=0
120 FOR Y=30 TO 1 STEP −2
130 PRINT AT X, Y; "AT";
140 LET Z=Z+1
150 PRINT TAB Z; "T"
160 NEXT Y
170 NEXT X
```

RUN this program a few times. (It must be run in **SLOW** mode.) Notice that the T's (printed by the statement with **TAB**) begin printing on the line following the AT's. When the TAB number is less than the column number for the **AT**, the T is printed in the column of the line following the print position. When the AT's and T's cross, though, the print position has a lower column number than the one given in the **TAB** command, so that the T's print on the same line as the AT's. Watch the program carefully until you can see this.

One additional command changes the display: the **SCROLL** command. **SCROLL** erases the top line of the screen and moves everything up one line.

Add this line to the program. (The **SCROLL** keyword is above the B key.)

155 SCROLL

Now **RUN** the program. The T's and AT's run in diagonal lines going up the screen because the AT values refer to absolute screen locations. In other words, after each AT is printed, all the lines move up the screen. but AT still prints on the same line. Since the previous content of that line is moved up, a diagonal pattern is formed.

PLOT, UNPLOT, AND GRAPHICS

When you looked at the characters in the last section, you may have noticed that there were several gray and black figures. These are the graphics characters. You will see these characters printed on 20 of the keys.

You may also have noticed that each of the other characters (except the keywords) appeared in two forms: the normal black character on a white background, and the inverse of a white character on a black background. (The inverse space is a black box.) The cursors are examples of inverse characters when the computer is in graphics mode.

The 9 key is labeled **GRAPHICS** in red. Hold the **SHIFT** key and press the 9. The word *graphics* did not appear; instead, the ▇ cursor changed to a ▇ cursor. That indicates that the computer is in *graphics mode*. Now type any character; it appears as a white character in a black box, just like the cursor. If you type G, you will see a duplicate of the ▇ cursor. Try typing G, K, and L. These characters look just like the three cursors. If you type an S, it will look just like the syntax error marker. Press the **SPACE** key. A black box appears. These are all inverse characters, since they are the opposite of the way characters usually appear.

Now hold the **SHIFT** key and press the Y key. Two small boxes appear, arranged diagonally. These are actually pictured on the Y key. Twenty of the keys have pictures labeled on them, each with a different pattern inside a box. Hold the **SHIFT** key down and type them all. When the computer is in graphics mode (that is, when the ▇ cursor is displayed), pressing **SHIFT** and typing one of the keys with graphics characters causes the graphics character to appear on the TV. If any of the characters is typed without the **SHIFT** key, the inverse version of that character appears. If you press the **SHIFT** key and type any of the keys that do not have graphics characters on them, the inverse version of the character in red is printed. Try holding **SHIFT** and pressing the comma key, for example.

To leave the graphics mode, press **SHIFT**/9; the ◼ cursor returns. Type **SHIFT**/P to close the quotation. Now press **ENTER**. The string of graphics characters (which you just typed) appears on the top of the screen, looking as it did inside the quotation marks.

You may use graphics characters in **PRINT** statements or in strings, but not in variable names.

One pair of statements is very important in creating graphic images on your TV. These are **PLOT** and **UNPLOT**. Type this command:

PLOT 10,10

A small black box, a quarter the size of a regular character, appears on the TV. **PLOT** simply displays one of these boxes at the location "10 over and 10 down". **UNPLOT** displays a white box, in effect erasing any black box located at the location you give. Type **NEW** to clear memory, and enter this program. (This program must be run in **SLOW** mode.)

```
10 PLOT 20,20
20 UNPLOT 20,20
30 GOTO 10
```

RUN the program. It just produces a flashing spot on the screen. To stop the program, hit the **BREAK** key.

For another example, enter this program:

```
10 PRINT "ENTER A ROW"
20 INPUT X
30 CLS
40 PRINT "ENTER A COLUMN"
50 INPUT Y
55 CLS
60 PLOT X,Y
70 GOTO 10
```

RUN it and try entering some numbers. If you enter a number greater than 64 for the row and 43 for the column, the program will "crash" because those numbers will be off the screen. Notice that the numbers go from the lower left corner, which is 0,0, to the upper right corner, which is 64,43. This is quite different from the position designations used for PRINT AT, where 0/0 is in the *upper* left corner. (Also, the numbers are twice as large, since each character position can hold four PLOTs—two in the row direction, and two in the column direction.

Also notice that anything printed immediately after the PLOT begins just after the PLOT position; this is because the PRINT position is moved by PLOT.

The Sketching game in Chapter 8 uses PLOT and UNPLOT in a way you may find interesting.

Here is one more program using PLOT. This must be run in SLOW mode.

```
10 PLOT 63*RND, 43*RND
20 GOTO 10
```

This program will run until stopped. Use the BREAK key when you are tired of watching.

FOR/NEXT LOOPS

Frequently a group of statements must be repeated a specific number of times. BASIC accomplishes this with the FOR ... NEXT statements.

Let's suppose you want to print your name ten times. You could do it with the following statements.

```
10 LET A=1
20 IF A>10 THEN GOTO 60
30 PRINT A, "BOZO"
40 LET A=A+1
50 GOTO 20
60 STOP
```

This program first checks to see if A is greater than 10; if not, it prints out the value of A, then your name, then jumps back to line 20. This process continues until, in line 20, A is greater than 10. The program than stops, because A is equal to 11.

A **FOR/NEXT** loop works in the same way these statements do. Enter the following statements. (Don't forget that **TO** is a keyword you type with **SHIFT/4.**)

```
10 FOR A=1 TO 10
20
40 NEXT A
50
```

The 20 and the 50 were typed on lines by themselves, replacing the previous lines of the same number from the program; line 30 was left alone.

Now **RUN** this program.

The results are exactly the same as in the first version of this program.

Let's go back to the first version to illustrate more about **FOR/NEXT** loops. Type these statements in:

```
10 LET A=10
20 IF A<1 THEN GOTO 60
40 LET A=A-1
50 GOTO 20
```

Notice that this time the loop counter starts at 10, and its value decreases by 1 each time around the loop. When the value of A becomes less than one, the program terminates.

Before looking at an equivalent **FOR/NEXT** loop, let's try one more example:

```
10 LET A=0
20 IF A>1 THEN GOTO 60
40 LET A=A+.2
```

Leave the rest of the program the same and **RUN** this version. This time, the loop counter starts at 0 and rises by .2 until it reaches 1. Your name is printed six times.

The value .2 in this example (−1 in the previous example, and 1 in the examples before that) is known as the *step value* of the loop. During each step through the loop, the step value is added to the loop counter until the loop counter's value is greater than the termination value defined in the **IF** statement.

Unless you declare otherwise, the step value in a **FOR** statement is 1. You can also define the initial and termination values to be anything you want.

The general format for a **FOR** statement is:

> **FOR** variable name = initial value **TO** final value
> [**STEP** VALUE]

The part in brackets, the keyword **STEP** and the step value, is optional. If you don't give them, the value 1 is always used. If the **STEP** value is negative, the initial value of the loop counter should be greater than the termination value. A negative step value requires the initial value to be larger than the final value, In this way you can write programs that "count down."

IF . . . THEN COMMANDS
AND RELATIONAL EXPRESSIONS

IF . . . THEN statements all have the same form. **IF** some mathematical relationship is true, **THEN** execute this command. If the mathematical relationship is false, do the next statement in the program.

There are six possible relationships that can be tested in an **IF . . . THEN** conditional statement. They are:

Relationship	Symbol
greater than	>
less than	<
equal to	=
greater than or equal to	> =
less than or equal to	< =
not equal to	< >

You may chain relationships together, using the keywords **AND** and **OR** (**SHIFT/2** and **SHIFT/W**).

Consider the following statement:

```
65 IF (NUMBER>GUESS AND NUMBER-10<=
GUESS) OR (NUMBER<GUESS AND NUMBER+10
>=GUESS) THEN PRINT "BUT YOU ARE CLOSE"
```

Statement 65 is made up of two sets of relationships. Each set of relationships is, in turn, made of two separate relationships. When the computer executes statement 65, it first checks whether NUMBER is greater than GUESS. If it is greater, the computer checks whether 10 less than NUMBER is still greater (NUMBER − 10 < = GUESS). Since the two relationships are connected with AND, the two together are true only if both are true.

Similarly, the second set is true only if both parts are true. The first set of relationships is connected to the second set with an OR keyword, however, so if either of the sets is true, the IF statement is true and the THEN command is executed.

In general terms, when AND connects two relationships, both must be true for the two together to be true. When OR connects two relationships, if one of the two is true (or if both are), then the two together are true.

Conditionals also apply to strings:

IF "JON" > "JOHN" THEN PRINT "JON"

The computer prints JON because the internal code for JON is a higher number than the internal code for JOHN. The computer compares the names, letter by letter. The first two letters, J and O, are the same in both names. The third letter of JON is N, and the third letter of JOHN is H. The code for N is 51, while the code for H is 45. Therefore, JON is greater than JOHN.

Strings may be compared in all the ways numbers may be compared. In all cases, the first letter (from the left) where the two strings differ is the determining factor.

We have been talking as if the computer recognizes the concepts "true" and "false." In fact, the computer actually uses numbers to represent these concepts. Try typing this command.

PRINT 1.5>.9

The computer prints a 1 on the top of the screen.

Type this command:

PRINT 1.5 < .9

The computer prints a zero on the screen.

When a relationship is true, the computer assigns the value 1 in place of the relationship. When a relationship is false, the computer assigns the value 0 in place of the relationship.

You can use this feature in many ways. For example, try typing the following statements:

```
50 GOTO 60+10*(NUMBER>GUESS)
60 PRINT "TOO HIGH"
65 GOTO 20
70 PRINT "TOO LOW"
75 GOTO 20
```

Run the program to see that it works the same as the original program. (The line that tells you whether you are close has been taken out to make the example simpler.)

What makes the program work now is line 50, the **GOTO** statement. If NUMBER is greater than GUESS, the expression NUMBER > GUESS is given the value 1. Since 60 + (10*1) = 70, the program jumps to line 70. If NUMBER is less than GUESS, the expression NUMBER > GUESS is equal to 0, and 60 + (10×0) = 60, so the program jumps to line 60.

As you write more programs, you will begin to find that the T/S 1000's small amount of memory is the biggest limitation to what your programs can accomplish. Techniques like this one reduce the size of programs and help you do more with the computer.

FUNCTIONS

Some program operations must be performed frequently. Instead of requiring every program actually to perform these operations, the T/S 1000 has predefined routines called *functions* that do the operation for the program.

With one exception, **RND**, all of the functions take a value, and return a second value that depends on the first. The first value is called the *argument* of the function. For example, consider this command:

PRINT INT A

Here the variable A is the argument of the function **INT**.

The argument of a function can be a variable, a constant, or an expression. However, since functions are evaluated before mathematical operators (+, −, *, /, and **), you should put the expression in parentheses. For example, try typing these two commands:

PRINT INT (1+.34)
PRINT INT 1+.34

In the first, the computer adds the 1 and .34 together, and then takes the **INT** of 1.34. In the second command, the computer first takes the **INT** of 1 and then adds that to .34, yielding 1.34.

Many functions require string arguments. These functions, **CODE**, **VAL**, and **LEN**, all produce numeric results. **VAL** evaluates the contents of the string as if it were a numeric expression. The string must therefore contain only items that would be legal in a numeric expression. For example, type the following statements. (First enter **NEW** to clear memory.)

```
10 PRINT "INPUT AN EXPRESSION"
20 INPUT A$
30 PRINT VAL A$
40 GOTO 20
```

RUN the program, entering any legal numeric expression. The expression you give is stored in the string variable A$. The **VAL** of A$ is then printed. Because the results are exactly equivalent, you can think of **VAL** as removing the quotation marks from the expression. Note, though, that **VAL** cannot evaluate a string that would not be legal in a numeric expression. The following statements, for example, would *not* work:

```
10 LET A$ = "HELLO"
20 VAL A$
```

To end the program, **DELETE** the left quotation mark and give the command **STOP**.

The function **LEN** returns the length of a string. When applied to a string, **LEN** returns the number of characters in the string.

CODE returns the number that is used internally by the computer to represent the first character in a string. All characters used by the computer are numbered according to an internal coding system, ranging from 0 to 255. A, for example, is 38. B is 39. The character 1 has the internal code 29. These codes are listed in a chart in the manual that came with your computer. Try this program. (First type **NEW** to clear memory.)

```
10 INPUT A$
20 PRINT CODE A$
30 GOTO 10
```

You can find out the code of any character with this program. Notice that if you give more than one character, all characters after the first are ignored. To end the program, **DELETE** the left quotation mark and give the **STOP** command.

The opposite of **CODE** is the **CHR$** function. It produces the character whose code is the argument of **CHR$**. Enter this program:

```
10 FOR X=0 TO 255
20 PRINT CHR$ X;
30 NEXT X
```

This program prints out the entire set of characters used by the T/S 1000. Spaces filled by question marks either are nonprinting characters (**ENTER**, for example) or are unused. Notice that as a memory conservation measure, all keywords are stored internally as single characters.

Perhaps the most unusual function is **INKEY$**. This function returns a single character which is the key being pressed at the keyboard when **INKEY$** was executed. If no key is pressed, **INKEY$** returns an empty string. See the Sketching game in Chapter 8 for a good example of the use of **INKEY$**.

π (PI) is a constant, not a function, but it is worth mentioning here. Enter the following command:

PRINT PI

Note that when you press the key which says π (**SHIFT/ENTER** to get the ▇ cursor, then the M key), PI is displayed on the screen. The value printed is simply the value of π, a very important constant in mathematics. For example, the next program prints the circumference of any circle. You should enter the radius of the circle. (The radius is the distance from the center of the circle to one edge—half of the diameter. The circumference is the distance around the edge of the circle.)

```
10 PRINT "GIVE A RADIUS"
20 INPUT RADIUS
30 PRINT 2*PI*RADIUS
```

Two other functions are very useful: **ABS** and **SGN**. **ABS** returns the absolute value of the argument. This means that if the argument is positive, the same number is returned. If the argument is negative, the negative sign is stripped off, and the rest of the number is returned. **SGN** simply tells you whether a number is positive, negative, or zero. It returns a 1 if the number is positive, a -1 if the number is negative, and a 0 if the number is zero.

The other functions will prove very useful on occasion. After you finish working through this book, you may want to look at the descriptions of functions in the manual that came with your computer, so that you know what is available.

SCIENTIFIC NOTATION

Occasionally you might see a number like this:

2.432902E+18

This number may look odd. It is written in a computer's version of *scientific notation*, which is a shorthand way of writing very large numbers. The E embedded in the number means "times 10 raised to the power," so the number is equal to:

2.432902*10**18

If you feel more comfortable with the common form of exponents, here's the same number again:

$2.432902*10^{18}$

Because you can convert it to ordinary notation simply by moving the decimal point 18 places to the right, this is a convenient short cut for writing huge numbers.

The number above is equal to 2,432,902,000,000,000,000, a number too large to be easily grasped. When dealing with numbers this large, seeing them in scientific notation makes them easier to comprehend. In addition, it saves memory.

This type of notation is also used when the number is very, very small. Notice in the E number above that the exponent (18) is preceded by a plus sign (+). If it were preceded by a minus sign (−), then you would move the decimal point to the left the indicated number of places. For example, enter this command:

PRINT 2**−20

The answer the computer printed out was:

9.5367432E−7

That is equivalent to .00000095367432, which is a very small number.

In the computer version of scientific notation, 5E−10 is equal to 5*1/10E10.

7

Dice Revisited

IMPROVING THE DICE PROGRAM

```
70 PRINT "HOW MANY DICE TO ROLL?"
100 INPUT A
200 CLS
300 IF A=0 THEN STOP
500 PRINT INT (1+6 * RND)
600 LET A=A−1
700 GOTO 300
```

Our old friend, the dice program from Chapter 4, is not bad considering what you set out to accomplish. You could use it to play craps, for example. Chances are, though, your friends won't be very impressed. The TV display consists entirely of a couple of numbers. It would be a much better show if the program actually displayed an image of the dice themselves.

It is not necessary to start over from scratch. Your dice program is a good central routine we can build on. Let's re-write our original three-point plan, adding some new points to enhance the program.

1. Find out how many dice player wants to "roll." If player enters a zero here, this signals end of program.
2. Program randomly chooses a die side.
3. Repeat step 2 the number of times indicated by player in step 1.
4. Display the dice faces graphically on the screen.
5. Return program execution to step 1.

We accomplished the first three objectives of our plan in Chapter 4. In addition to the new objectives, let's also apply a new programming technique: the **FOR . . . NEXT** loop. Some explanation is provided here, but our improvements will be much easier to understand if you've already read the previous chapter.

The most obvious way to improve the program is to replace the somewhat clumsy line 600 with a more streamlined **FOR . . . NEXT** loop. As you will see, it also allows us to satisfy point 5 in our plan. A **FOR** statement says, "Perform the following statements a certain number of times." **NEXT** defines the end of the loop.

These are the statements in the program:

```
400 FOR X=1 TO A
600 NEXT X
700 GOTO 70
```

The **FOR** statement creates the loop. The variable, X, is called the *loop counter*. You may select any single letter as the loop counter variable. When the computer executes the **FOR** statement for the first time, it creates the variable X (if one exists already, it is destroyed), then sets its value equal to the number after the equal sign (in this case, 1). This is the initial value of the loop counter. The computer then proceeds through the program until it reaches **NEXT** X. At this point, the computer adds a 1 to the value X and checks to see whether X has reached a value greater than A. If X is not greater than A, the program goes through the loop again.

Loop counters are somewhat different from other variables. They must always be named with a single letter. You can use their value in the middle of a loop (in fact, that is one of the most powerful things about **FOR/NEXT** loops), but you generally should not change their value.

The simple addition of these three lines allows us to accomplish point 5. Now program execution proceeds automatically to line 700, after which the player once again enters a number and is also given the opportunity to terminate the program by entering 0.

Now it's time to attack the problem of graphic display. First, however, we must take a side trip to learn about a very important part of programming: arrays.

An *array* is simply a group of variables that all go under the same general name. The statement

DIM D$(6,9)

creates an array containing six string variables: D$(1), D$(2), D$(3), D$(4), D$(5), and D$(6). Each variable in the array is called an *array element*. The second number in the **DIM** statement, 9, is the string length of each of the elements in the array.

A string array element is exactly like any other string variable except that the array element has a defined length. An ordinary string variable can hold a string of any length, and the variable grows or shrinks to hold any string you try to put in it. When you define a string variable or an array with a **DIM** statement, however, the variable or array element stays at the defined size. If you try to put too long a string into the element, the element will accept only what it can hold—the rest of the string is lost.

You can use a **DIM** statement to give a simple string variable a fixed length. In that case, you use a command like **DIM** A$(5). After that, A$ always holds just five characters.

Numeric arrays are different from string arrays in that you never define a "length" for a numeric array. Numeric array elements are exactly like ordinary numeric variables, except they are named with a single letter.

DIM D$(6,9) defines a string array with six elements. Each element can hold nine characters. (By comparison, **DIM** X(6) defines a numeric array named X with 6 elements. As always, each element can hold one number, although the number can be very large.)

Here are the new lines to create our graphics:

```
5 DIM D$(6,9)
10 LET D$(1) = "****O****"
20 LET D$(2) = "***O*O***"
30 LET D$(3) = "O***O***O"
```

```
40 LET D$(4) = "O*O***O*O"
50 LET D$(5) = "O*O*O*O*O"
60 LET D$(6) = "O*OO*OO*O"
```

Line 5 creates a string array with six elements, each of which can hold up to 9 characters. The six assignment statements in the program assign strings to be used to represent dice. Look closely at the strings. If three characters are taken at a time and laid on top of each other, an image is created that looks like the face of a die. This is what the string in line 30 looks like, "sliced and stacked":

```
O**  ← first 3 characters of D$(1)
*O*  ← middle 3 characters of D$(1)
**O  ← last 3 characters of D$(1)
```

So far you haven't typed a single line into the program to display dice. If you add the following statements, the program will work. (Type the keyword **STEP** with **SHIFT**/E. Type the keyword **TO** with **SHIFT**/4.)

```
500 LET B=INT (1+6 * RND)
510 FOR Y=1 TO 9 STEP 3
520 PRINT D$(B,Y TO Y+2)
530 NEXT Y
540 PRINT
```

The new statement 500 is much like the old statement 500, except that the random value is saved in a new variable, B, instead of being printed directly.

Statement 510 is similar to the **FOR** loop you have already seen. The difference is the **STEP** keyword. Without **STEP**, the **NEXT** statement adds 1 to the loop variable. With **STEP**, the **NEXT** statement adds the number following **STEP** to the loop variable.

Statement 520, the **PRINT** statement, is the key statement in this new version of the program. Here it is again:

```
520 PRINT D$(B,Y TO Y+2)
```

B is the random value between 1 and 6 chosen in statement 500. For the entire **FOR** loop, this **PRINT** statement will print data from the chosen line of the array 510–530. If you look closely at the **FOR** statement, you will see that it will execute three times. The first time, the loop variable Y will be equal to 1. The second time, the loop variable will be equal to 4. The third time, Y will have the value 7.

Therefore, when the **PRINT** statement is executed, it will use the following values:

```
PRINT D$(B,1 TO 3)
PRINT D$(B,4 TO 6)
PRINT D$(B,7 TO 9)
```

Just as you mentally "sliced" the strings into three pieces in order to see how the strings added up to die faces, the "number **TO** number" clauses in these **PRINT** statements take slices of the string. This slicing technique can be used anywhere a string or string variable can be used, even on the left side of a **LET** statement's equal sign. For example, type these commands:

```
DIM A$(12)
LET A$(1 TO 3)="HEL"
LET A$(4 TO 6)="LO,"
LET A$(7 TO 10)="THE"
LET A$(11 TO 12)="RE"
PRINT A$
```

The message HELLO, THERE is written on the TV.

Statement 540, the **PRINT** which is alone on a line, is used to get a blank line between die faces.

Let it be a programming challenge for you to further enhance the dice program by making the dice appear at random locations on the screen.

8
Game Programs

SOLVING CROSSWORD PUZZLES

If you work crossword puzzles, you probably have days when you just can't come up with a word to fit in the space allotted. This program may be just what you need on those days.

Enter your word, putting in dashes where there is a letter missing. The program then randomly adds letters and prints the results on the screen. It will continue until the screen is filled. If you want to continue, enter **CONT**. You then get another screenful of words.

Run this in **SLOW** mode. It works fairly quickly, and you are more likely to see the word you want if you watch while the computer is displaying the words. If you try to scan a screenful at a time, you might well miss the word you need.

If your word is missing only one letter, then you will see all 26 combinations and the program is fine. If the word is missing two letters, there are 676 combinations. If it is missing three letters, there are 17,576 combinations, and there isn't much chance you will see the one you need. We'll suggest a modification to get around that problem; first, here is the basic program:

```
100 PRINT "WORD?"
110 INPUT A$
120 LET B$=A$
130 FOR X=2 TO LEN A$
140 IF B$(X) = "—" THEN LET B$(X) = CHR$
    INT (CODE "A" +RND *26)
150 NEXT X
160 PRINT B$ +" ";
170 GOTO 120
```

The program stores the original word in B$, and then alters the B$ copy in the **FOR/NEXT** loop. Whenever a dash (—) is found in B$, it is replaced with a randomly chosen letter. That choosing process is the heart of this program and is worth looking at in more detail. The expression

CHR$ INT (CODE "A"+RND*26)

is used to choose one of the 26 letters. The expression within parentheses chooses a number between 38 (which is the internal code for A) and 63 (the internal code for Z). Since **RND** always produces a number between 0 and 1, a value that can sometimes equal 0 but is always less than 1, multiplying **RND** by 26 ensures that the value is between 0 and 26, and it may sometimes take the value 0, but will always be less than 26. Adding the value of **CODE** "A", which is 38, produces a number between 38 and 63.99999999. (Using **CODE** "A" instead of the number 38 saves a little space and makes the purpose of the expression clearer.) Taking the **INT** of that value produces a number between 38 and 63, inclusive. The function **CHR$** returns the string character with the code value of the argument of **CHR$**. Therefore, the expression results in a randomly chosen letter.

Statement 160 prints the words obtained, adding blank spaces between words.

As mentioned before, this program is practical if your word is missing one letter or if you have absolutely no idea what the word could be. It might, then, come up with the answer, or at least give you some ideas.

If you reduce the number of choices for the missing letters, you increase the program's chances of finding the word.

You can add these statements to the program:

```
115 PRINT "LETTERS?"
116 INPUT L$
140 IF A$(X)="—" THEN LET B$(X)=
    L$(INT(1+RND*LEN L$))
```

The new line 140 is like the old one, except in the way the random letter is chosen. Here, a random number is chosen that is between 1 and the length of the string of characters you typed in. (The function **LEN** returns the length of a string. When the length of the string is not fixed by a **DIM** statement, it is determined by the number of characters in the string.) So the expression L$(INT(1+ RND*LEN L$)) names one of the letters you used. Writing the program this way would be especially useful, for instance, if you knew the word was missing only vowels.

HI-LO

When a computer seems so clever that you would swear it was intelligent, rest assured: the apparent "intelligence" is only the result of cleverly written **IF . . . THEN** statements.

These statements and other statements using relational expressions allow computers to make decisions. These are called *conditional expressions*. They simply say, as in English, "If one thing is true, then do such-and-such."

Enter the following program. **INT** and **RND** are function keywords. You must press **SHIFT/ENTER** to get the ▣ cursor in order to type them. After you type the **THEN** keyword (**SHIFT**/3), the ▣ cursor will be displayed and you can type the command keywords **GOTO** and **PRINT**. Each **IF** statement will spill over onto a second line. Don't worry about that —the computer doesn't care how long statements are and will simply start printing on a second line once you fill up the first.

```
10 LET NUMBER=INT (RND*100)
20 PRINT "GUESS?"
30 INPUT GUESS
40 IF NUMBER=GUESS THEN GOTO 80
50 IF NUMBER>GUESS THEN PRINT "TOO LOW"
60 IF NUMBER<GUESS THEN PRINT "TOO HIGH"
65 IF (NUMBER>GUESS AND NUMBER-10<=
GUESS) OR (NUMBER<GUESS AND NUMBER+10
>=GUESS) THEN PRINT "BUT YOU ARE CLOSE"
70 GOTO 20
80 PRINT "YOU WIN"
```

Try running it. The program picks a random whole number between 0 and 100. The player is supposed to guess it. If the number is not correctly guessed before the screen is full (the program stops with a report code of 5/20), give the **CONT** command (press the C key) to clear the screen; the program will continue.

ZENO'S PARADOX

Zeno's logical paradox is that in order to walk across the room, you must first walk halfway across the room, then walk half the remaining distance, and then walk half of the remaining quarter of the room, and then walk half of the distance still left, and so on. Theoretically, if you keep walking only half the distance each time, you will never get there!

This program calculates the time required to go 100 feet, to within a quarter-inch of the destination. For the sake of simplicity, let's assume that it takes 1 second to cross each half distance.

```
10 LET A=100*12*4
20 LET B=0
30 LET A=A/2
40 LET B=B+1
50 IF A>2 THEN GOTO 30
60 PRINT "IT TOOK ";B;" SECONDS"
```

Statement 10 figures out how many quarter-inches are in 100 feet. Statements 30 through 50 form a loop, which divides the distance in half, adds a second to the time, then checks to see if there is less than a quarter-inch left. (Since the distance was converted to quarter-inches, 1 is one quarter-inch.)

That didn't take very long. It assumes that a quarter-inch is close enough, though.

The smallest number the T/S 1000 can handle is slightly smaller than 1 E−38. E means "times 10 to the power," so that number is equal to 1 times 10^{-38}, or .0000000000000000000000000000000000000001, a very small number indeed.

Change line 50 to look like this:

```
50 IF A>1 E−38 THEN GOTO 30
```

Then run the program, to see how long it will take to get this close.

SPACE BLASTER

Welcome to the space fleet! You have received a tough assignment, near the center of the galaxy, patrolling a small sector.

This remote sector is inhabited by a monster. The monster will eat your ship in an instant if it gets a chance. Fortunately, you have a mine with which to blow up the monster. Unfortunately, the monster is immortal. When you blow the monster up, it immediately appears again somewhere else in your sector.

As an additional problem, your mine isn't very cooperative. Your ship is too small to carry the mine itself, so the mine is teleported from your home base, an asteroid at one corner of your sector. Space behaves oddly this close to the galactic center: the mine won't stay put, but keeps returning to base. At the beginning of your patrol, the mine returns to base almost immediately. As time goes on, the mine is more cooperative and stays longer.

You can use the mine to avoid the monster for a while (if you are clever and lucky enough), but your only real hope is to get back to your base, where the mine will protect you continuously. Watch out, though. Space is warped near your base: if you touch the edge of the field, you may not be where you think you are and your directional controls may act strangely.

Here is the program:

```
10 DIM X(2)
20 DIM O(2)
```

```
 30 DIM S(2)
 40 LET X(1)=5
 50 LET X(2)=1
 60 LET O(1)=20
 70 LET O(2)=O (1)
 80 LET SCORE=0
 90 LET TIME=0
100 LET SAFE=0
200 CLS
210 PRINT AT X(1), X(2); "X"
220 PRINT AT O(1), O(2); "O"
230 IF O(1)=X(1) AND O(2) =X(2) THEN GOTO
    1000
240 LET M$=INKEY$
250 IF M$="5" OR M$="8" THEN LET O(2)=
    Ø(2)+SGN (VAL M$-7)
260 IF M$="6" OR M$="7" THEN LET O(1)=
    O(1)-2*VAL M$+13
270 IF M$ < >"S" THEN GOTO 300
280 LET S(1)=O(1)
290 LET S(2)=O(2)
300 IF INT (TIME/10)< >INT (RND*TIME/10)
    THEN GOTO 330
310 LET S(1)=0
320 LET S(2)=0
330 LET TIME=TIME+1
340 PRINT AT S(1), S(2); "S"
350 IF O(1)=Ø AND O(2)=0 THEN LET SAFE=
    SAFE+1
360 IF SAFE> =10 THEN GOTO 1000
370 LET X(1)=X(1)+SGN (O(1)-X(1))
380 LET X(2)=X(2)+SGN (O(2)-X(2))
390 IF X(1)< >S(1) OR X(2)< >S(2) THEN GOTO
    200
400 LET SCORE=SCORE+1
410 LET X(1)=INT (RND*22)
420 LET X(2)=INT (RND*32)
430 GOTO 200
1000 PRINT "SCORE IS"; SCORE+SAFE
```

RUN this program in SLOW mode, using the keys with arrows to move your spaceship around. (Your ship is the

O.) Don't press **SHIFT** to use the arrow keys the way you usually would; just press the keys alone. Your home base is in the upper left corner. You can see the mine there—it's that graphic symbol. To get the mine to your ship's location, press the S key. You can't move and retrieve the mine simultaneously, so you must let go of the arrow keys while you press the S. The mine will come to your ship's location and stay there (even if you move the ship) for a period of time that is very short at the beginning of the game but gets longer as you play.

The monster (the X) chases you. Its speed is faster than yours when it is moving diagonally, but its speed is the same as yours when it is moving vertically or horizontally. You don't have much chance of keeping away from the creature; you have to use the mine to protect yourself. When the monster runs into the mine, it disappears, and reappears in some random place. You score a point every time the monster runs into the mine. If you make it to home base, the game counts for ten moves, and then ends. You get ten points for ending the game without being eaten.

Here's how the program works. Three arrays, X, O, and S, store the positions of the monster, your ship, and the mine, respectively. The statements before 200 set up the variables used in the program. TIME keeps track of how long the game has been going on. SAFE keeps track of how long you are safely in your base.

The display is redrawn after each move to update the positions. Statements 210 and 220 display you and the monster. If you are in the same position, the monster has eaten you, and statement 230 causes a jump to the end of the program.

Statement 240 gets your move, using the **INKEY$** function. This function recognizes any key being pressed at the keyboard.

Statement 250 finds out if the 5 or 8 key is being pressed. These are the keys with left and right arrows on them. If one of them is pressed while line 250 is executing, the expression SGN (**VAL** M$−7) is used to determine the new position. SGN returns a −1 if the argument is negative and a 1 if the argument is positive. **VAL** converts a string into a number with the same characters and so converts the string "5" to a number 5, and the string "8" to a number 8. Subtracting 7 from those numbers yields a negative number if the key was 5 (left arrow), or a positive number if the key was 8 (right arrow). The result is to subtract 1 from the column if the left arrow is pressed and add 1 if the right arrow is pressed.

Statement 260 performs a similar action for the up and down arrow keys, although it used a different method. Since the up arrow key is 7 and the down arrow key is 6, the value of the key is doubled and made negative, and the result is added to 13. A 6 (down arrow) yields a +1, which is added to the row. A 5 (down arrow), would yield a −1, which is also added to the row.

Statement 270 checks to see if the pressed key was S. If so, the mine is moved to the current ship position by setting S(1) equal to X(1) and S(2) equal to O(2).

Statement 300 compares a randomly chosen number with INT (TIME/10); if equal, the mine is moved back to home base. Then 1 is added to TIME. The mine is displayed by line 340.

Line 350 checks to see if your ship is in home base. If it is, then a 1 is added to your SAFE time. If SAFE is equal to 10, line 360 ends the game.

Lines 370 and 380 cause the monster to chase your ship. Your ship's position is subtracted from the monster's position, and the SGN function is applied to the result. The monster then moves one row and one column toward your ship.

Line 390 checks to see if the monster has run into the mine. If it has, you score a point, and the monster's position is randomly reassigned by statements 410 and 420.

Statement 430 loops back for another move.

Finally, statement 1000 is the program terminator. It prints out your score, which is the total of the number of times the monster ran into your mines, and the amount of time you were in home base.

One operating note: the moves get strange when you run into the left side or the top of the screen because the "position" of the ship becomes negative. PRINT AT uses the absolute value of the position given, so the negative positions are translated into positive positions, but the arrow keys work in reverse directions. If you go too far on the bottom or right sides of the screen, however, the program will "crash."

COIN FLIP

The **RND** (random number) function on the T/S 1000, as on all computers, actually produces a pseudorandom number. "Pseudorandom" instead of "random" indicates that it is merely a simulation of a random number. The computer uses a formula normally based on the amount of time the computer has been switched on. The numbers produced are random enough for most purposes, but they may not be as random as some physical events, like the tossing of a coin.

When you toss a coin, you expect it to come up heads as often as tails. That doesn't mean that it will *always* come up heads as often as tails, just that if you flip the coin enough times, you can expect an aproximately equal number of heads and tails.

Try typing in this program:

```
10 FAST
20 DIM B(2)
30 FOR X=1 TO 10
40 LET A=1+RND
50 LET B(A)=B(A)+1
60 NEXT X
70 PRINT B(1), B(2)
80 PRINT ABS (B(1)-B(2))*100/ (B(2)+B(2));
   "PERCENT"
```

RND produces a number between 0 and 1. Therefore, the number should be between 0 and .5 half the time, and between .5 and 1 half the time. Adding 1 to **RND**, as in statement 40, yields a number between 1 and 1.5 half the time, and between 1.5 and 2 half the time. Notice that the **INT** function is not applied to **RND** in this program. When the computer expects an integer and gets a number with a decimal, it rounds the number off to the *nearest* integer. This is different from **INT**, which removes the decimal portion and always returns a number with a value lower than the original number. When the computer rounds off a number, if the decimal part is greater than .5, the computer replaces the number with the next higher integer. If the decimal part is less than .5, the computer replaces the number with the next lower integer, just as **INT** would.

The function **ABS**, used in line 80, returns the absolute value of B(1)−B(2). If the result is positive, **ABS** does nothing, if it is negative, **ABS** makes the number positive. Line 80 gives the percentage of difference between the two numbers. **RUN** the program a few times.

You will get numbers like 5 and 5, 6 and 4, 7 and 3. The difference between those numbers is 0%, 20%, and 40%. Notice that the percentage of difference may be large. If you flipped a coin only ten times, you wouldn't necessarily expect heads to come up five times and tails to come up five. Let's try the same thing with a hundred trials. Change line 30. You can retype the line, or use the **EDIT** key to change the 10 to 100.

The line should look like this:

```
30 FOR X=1 TO 100
```

Press **ENTER**, and the new line 30 replaces the old one.

RUN the program. It will take a few seconds. We got 56 and 44 (12%) the first time we ran this, 50 and 50 (0%) the second time, 57 and 43 (14%) the third time, 55 and 45 (10%) the fourth time, and 54 and 46 (8%) the fifth time. These numbers are fairly close, but it might be interesting to try this program with a thousand trials. Press **EDIT** to get line 30 back down to the **INPUT** line. (The **EDIT** cursor stays on the last line that was entered, in this case 30, unless you did something else in between.)

Now **RUN** the program again. (It takes 25 seconds to do 1,000 trials, so be patient.) We got 487 and 513 (2.2%) the first time we tried, and 477 and 523 (4.6%) the second time. The third time, we got 511 and 489 (2.2%), and 517 and 483 (3.4%) the fourth.

Notice that, although the numbers are never equal, they are getting proportionally closer as we increase the number of trials. That is a good sign. Real-life random numbers (coins, dice, roulette tables) also have their fluctuations. That is why you can beat the roulette table in a casino now and then. However, the odds are tilted so that the house has some advantage. If you want, try changing line 30 to this:

30 LET A=1.1+RND

The odds will now be tilted to make the second number come up more often. That is how casinos stay in business. They may lose occasionally, but over 365 days, with tens of thousands of spins of the roulette wheel and throws of the dice at the craps table, it all evens out—in their favor.

If you want to demonstrate that the numbers get closer to each other as the trials go up, try changing the number of trials to 10,000. This time, it will take almost five minutes for the program to finish running. When we ran the program through 10,000 trials, we got 5,028 and 4,972, which differ by only 0.56%. As the number of trials increases, the numbers certainly get closer.

SKETCHING

This program does a fair imitation of a child's sketching toy, with which you can draw on a blank panel by manipulating two knobs.

In this version, you use the arrows on the 5, 6, 7, and 8 keys to indicate your direction. Just press the keys—don't use the **SHIFT** key.

As an improvement over the children's toy, you can erase lines as well as draw them. The program begins in draw mode. To erase lines, press the **UNPLOT** key. You then erase with the arrow keys in the same way you draw. (However, you can see your position only when you cross a plotted line.)

Here is the program:

```
10 SLOW
20 LET X=25
30 LET Y=X
40 LET DRAW=1000
50 LET ERASE=2000
60 LET C=DRAW
70 PLOT X,Y
100 LET A$=INKEY$
110 IF A$="Q" THEN LET C=DRAW
120 IF A$="W" THEN LET C=ERASE
130 IF A$>="5" AND A$<="8" THEN GOTO
    100* (VAL A$)
140 GOTO 100
500 LET X=X−1
510 GOTO C
600 LET Y=Y−1
610 GOTO C
700 LET Y=Y+1
710 GOTO C
800 LET X=X+1
810 GOTO C
1000 PLOT X,Y
1010 GOTO 100
2000 UNPLOT X,Y
2010 GOTO 100
```

The statements preceding line 100 initialize the program; that is, they define the initial values of the program's variables. A plot mark (a box a quarter of the size of a character) is displayed at position 25. The variables DRAW and

ERASE are used for clarity. Their values are used later in switching between the draw and erase modes. The variable C, which is set to DRAW, remembers whether the program is in the draw (**PLOT**) mode or the erase (**UNPLOT**) mode. The program is put in **SLOW** mode in line 10 because it simply will not work in **FAST** mode.

The loop formed by statements 100 to 140 are the heart of the program. The **INKEY$** function returns a character if any key has been pressed. If no key has been pressed, **INKEY$** returns a null character. The statements 110, 120, and 130 take some action if a Q, W, 5, 6, 7, or 8 has been pressed. Q is the key labeled **PLOT**; W is labeled **UNPLOT**. When Q is pressed, the variable C is set to equal the variable DRAW (which is also C's initial value). When W is pressed, C is set equal to the variable ERASE. Statement 130 checks to see whether the **INKEY$** value (A$) is equal to 5, 6, 7, or 8, and if so, then jumps to a statement based on the value of A$. The statement to which it jumps is determined by the expression

100***VAL** A$

VAL returns a numerical value equivalent to the string A$. (See Chapter 6 for a detailed discussion of **VAL**.) If A$ contains a "5", **VAL** A$ returns the numerical value 5. Therefore, the command **GOTO** 100*VAL A$ jumps to 500 if the 5 (left arrow) key is pressed; 600 if the 5 (down arrow) key is pressed; and so on.

Each statement 500, 600, 700, and 800 adds or subtracts one from the X or Y values, as appropriate. Statements 510, 610, 710, and 810 then jump to the line number represented by the value C. C can be equal to either 1000 or 2000 (DRAW or ERASE), so, depending on the mode, these statements jump to lines 1000 or 2000. Line 1000 plots the point, line 2000 unplots (erases) the point. Statement 1010 and 2010 then jump back to 200, where the loop continues until another appropriate key is pressed.

Notice that the program could easily be written with statement 100 LET A$=INKEY$ replaced by an **INPUT** statement. However, the person using the program would then have to press **ENTER** each time in order to draw or erase a bit of a line.

PATTERNS

This program takes a number you enter and creates patterns from it. You must enter two-digit numbers for this program to run properly.

Here is the program:

```
10 PRINT "GIVE A NUMBER"
20 INPUT N
30 FOR K=1 TO N
40 LET R=22*K/N
50 LET A=P I*100*K/N
60 PLOT 32+R* COS A, 22+R*SIN A
70 NEXT K
80 GOTO 20
```

The "function" PI in line 50 produces the value 3.1415927. You type PI by pressing **SHIFT** and **ENTER**, to get the **F** cursor, and then pressing the M key, which has the PI symbol, π under it.

The program takes your number, then uses it to construct a picture based on a combination of the trigonometric functions. Once the picture is drawn, the program waits for another two numbers. To stop the program, enter a letter or another illegal value while the program is waiting for a number, or hit the **BREAK** key while the program is building a picture.

This program works better in **FAST** mode.

9

Educational Programs

ARITHMETIC DRILLS

This program selects two random numbers between 0 and 10, displays them with one of the arithmetic operators (+, −, *, or /), asks the student for an answer, then checks the answer. If the answer is wrong, the student gets another chance. If the anwer is right, there is a congratulatory display.

This is a basic teaching program. It could be altered to change the range of numbers used, allowing, for example,

numbers greater than 10, or exponentiation, or more complicated computations. You could also have the program supply the correct answer after the student has made a few
unsuccessful attempts. Even the congratulatory display
could be changed.

The secret to this program's operation is that wonderful
function, **VAL**. **VAL** evaluates a string as if it were a numeric expression. The program creates a string by generating two numbers, then using the string "+" operator to construct an equation out of the two numbers and a randomly
chosen operator. All of that is done in statement 200. Before
we explain more about the program, here it is:

```
50 DIM D$(4,1)
55 LET D$(1)="+"
60 LET D$(2)="−"
65 LET D$(3)="*"
70 LET D$(4)="/"
80 LET RIGHT=1000
90 FAST
100 LET A$=STR$ INT (RND*10)
150 LET B$=STR$ INT (1+RND*10)
200 LET E$=A$+D$ (INT (1+RND*4)) + B$
250 IF INT VAL E$ <> VAL E$ THEN GOTO 100
300 CLS
350 SLOW
400 PRINT E$;"=?"
450 INPUT A
500 IF A = VAL E$ THEN GOTO RIGHT
650 PRINT "SORRY. TRY AGAIN."
700 PAUSE 60
750 GOTO 400
1000 FOR X=1 TO 5
1050 SCROLL
1100 PRINT AT 21,0;
        "*********CONGRATULATIONS*********"
1150 NEXT X
1200 FOR X=1 TO 20
1250 SCROLL
1300 NEXT X
1350 GOTO 90
```

Line 80 might seem unfamiliar. The variable RIGHT is

used to hold the line number that begins the congratulatory message. The only reason to store the line number in a variable is to make the purpose of the **IF** statement on line 500 somewhat clearer. You can use a variable, an expression, or a constant in a **GOTO** or **GOSUB** statement.

The two lines that choose the numbers are slightly different. The first picks a number between 0 and 9. The second picks a number between 1 and 10. The limits are arbitrary, but they are arranged so that the second number is never a 0. Giving a 0 for the second number could result in a division by 0, which would cause the program to end.

Line 250 checks to make sure that the answer to the problem is an integer. That is also arbitrary. You could allow decimal fractions in the answer. However, there is the problem that a fraction such as 1/3 does not have an exact decimal answer, which might cause the program to reject a correct answer.

One disadvantage of this program is that it does not use the familiar symbols for division and multiplication. This should be explained beforehand. Another disadvantage is that the student can merely enter the original equation, and the computer will accept that as a correct answer. It is possible to restrict the answer to a simple one- or two-digit number by inserting these changes:

```
450 INPUT G$
460 IF LEN G$ > 2 THEN LET G$ = "999"
500 IF VAL G$ = VAL E$ THEN GOTO RIGHT
```

This limitation works because the largest number that can be produced by the program has only two digits. If more than two digits are found, it is counted as an incorrect answer.

Another point in this program is the use of **SLOW** and **FAST** modes. Calculations are done in **FAST** mode because it is about four times faster. Displaying is done in **SLOW** mode, which is more pleasing to the eye. You may find the flicker of **FAST** mode annoying, in which case it is wise to use **SLOW** whenever possible.

If you want to modify the limits of the equations generated by this program, all you have to do is change a few of the program statements. For example, to change the program to ask only addition and subtraction questions, you may add the following statements:

```
50 DIM D$(2,1)
65
70
200 LET B$ = STR$ INT (1+RND*2))+B$
```

(Typing 65 and 70 with nothing following them erases those lines from the program.)

Similarly, if you want to add the exponentiation operator (**), simply increase the number of elements in D$ to 5 by changing the 4 in line 50 to 5, add a statement to put ** into D$(5), and change the 1+RND*4 in line 200 to 1+RND*5.

If you want to change the limits of the numbers chosen, just change the 10s in lines 100 and 150 to whatever figure you choose. If you want to put other restrictions on the numbers, you can add IF statements. For example, if you want to make sure that the result is always positive, add the following line:

```
275 IF VAL E$<0 THEN GOTO 100
```

VOCABULARY

A teacher of high school English told us about a technique used to help teach children to write. The teachers select paragraphs, and cut out a word every so often, leaving blanks. The students then are asked to fill in the blanks with appropriate words.

This program automates the process of removing the words. Here it is:

```
10 LET C=1
20 PRINT "REMOVE HOW MANY WORDS?"
30 INPUT A
40 PRINT "ENTER PARAGRAPH"
50 INPUT A$
60 CLS
70 FOR X=1 TO LEN A$
80 IF A$ (X) <>" " THEN GOTO 100
90 LET C=C+1
100 IF C>A THEN LET C=1
110 IF C<A OR A$(X)=" " THEN GOTO 130
120 LET A$ (X)="?"
130 NEXT X
140 PRINT A$
```

The data entry part of it is straightforward. Since the string variable A$ is not dimensioned, your paragraph may be as long as you like. However, you must not use **ENTER** at the ends of lines. The computer automatically goes to the next line once you reach the end of a line. If this cuts up your words, you can add extra spaces, but the spaces will fool this program, making it count the words incorrectly.

Statement 80 searches for spaces. Every time it finds one, the program knows that it has just passed a word, and the word count (C) is increased by one. When the word count equals the REMOVE HOW MANY WORDS value given at the beginning of the program, the program looks for the next letter and replaces it with a question mark. The program continues replacing letters with question marks until it finds another space, which indicates the end of the word. When statement 80 finds the space at the end of the word, C is increased again by 1. When statement 100 finds that C (word count) is greater than A (remove word), it "resets" the value of C to 1 again, because the word count is supposed to start over again. Statement 110 finds that C is less than A, and skips statement 120.

You may notice that statement 120 would be skipped anyway, since the **OR** A$(X)="" in statement 110 would cause the **GOTO** to be executed. The **OR** clause is necessary to account for double spaces. If it wasn't there, the second space would be replaced by a question mark.

SPELLING BEE

The T/S 1000 is at a disadvantage in spelling drills because it cannot speak. This program gets around that problem by supplying partial words. You supply the program with as many as ten words (which can be up to ten letters long). You then specify how many letters should be removed from the words. The computer makes up the drill by picking one of the words at random, then replacing the proper number of randomly chosen letters with question marks. For example, suppose that one of the words you gave was ESTABLISH and that you asked the computer to remove two letters from each word. The computer might produce ES?ABLI?H. The student has to guess what word is meant. However, since the program is set up to give the student as many chances as required, the guessing can go on indefinitely. If the student finally gives up, the program prints the correct spelling of the word, then gives the student one wrong mark. If the student gets the word correctly, he or she gets one right mark and there is a little celebratory display.

Since this is quite a long program, it is listed here divided into sections, each of which has a separate function. The beginning of the program initializes the drill. Here it is.

```
1 SLOW
5 LET T=10
10 DIM C$(10)
15 DIM A$(T,10)
20 LET RT=0
```

```
25 LET WR=RT
30 PRINT "GIVE WORDS"
40 FOR X=1 TO T
50 INPUT A$(X)
60 IF A$(X)<"A" THEN GOTO 90
70 PRINT A$(X)
80 NEXT X
90 CLS
100 PRINT "REMOVE HOW MANY LETTERS?"
110 INPUT R
```

The display generally looks better in **SLOW** mode; in fact, the celebratory display will not work in **FAST** mode. Statement 5 sets the variable T equal to 10. Variable T is used to define the maximum number of words that can be used by the program. Notice that it is used in the statement defining the array A$ (which holds the words), and also in line 40, where it defines the termination value for the word input loop. It is also used later in the program. In each case, it is related to the maximum number of words used by the program. Using a variable in this way makes it easier to modify the program. If you want to change the maximum number of words the program can use, all you have to do is change the value assigned to T in statement 5.

Statement 15 **DIM** A$(T,10) sets the maximum length of words to 10 letters. That second value is not assigned to a variable, so changing the maximum word length is more difficult than changing the maximum number of words. As always, there is a tradeoff between keeping the program small and making the program easier to understand, alter, and fix.

Statement 10 dimensions the variable C$ to a fixed length of 10. C$ is used to accept the student's attempts to spell the word. The value of C$ is then compared with the original word to see if they match. Array elements *always* have a fixed length. If one of the words has less than 10 characters, then the rest of the array element holding that word is filled with blank spaces. If the student's answer was stored in an ordinary (un-**DIM**med) string variable, the variable would hold just the word, with no blank spaces. When the program tested to see whether the original word and the student's word matched, they would not, because the computer considers the blank spaces to be part of the word. Defining C$ always to have a length of 10 makes certain the student's answer also will be filled out to a length of 10.

The two variables defined in 20 and 25 hold the student's score. RT holds the number of right answers, and WR holds the number of wrong answers.

These initializing statements are followed by an input loop, which fills the array with the words supplied. As soon as a "null" word is supplied (that is, as soon you press **EN-TER**, without giving any letters), the program assumes that all words have been given, then "exits" from the input loop. You can always enter fewer than the maximum number of words. The null word is detected by statement 60, which compares the value entered to see if it is less than the value of an A.

When you use any of the relational operators ($<$, $>$, $>=$, $<=$, $=$, $<>$) with string values, the computer compares the codes for the *first* characters of each string. Line 60 of the program is meant to find out when the user has entered a "word" made of nothing but blanks. If so, it is assumed that the user does not want to add any more words to the list.

The second part of the program is the main operating section:

```
200 CLS
210 IF RT+WR>=20 THEN GOTO 1000
220 LET W=INT (1+RND*T)
230 IF A$(W)<"A" THEN GOTO 220
240 LET B$=A$ (W)
250 FOR X=1 TO R
260 LET N=INT (1+RND*10)
270 IF B$(N)<"A" THEN GOTO 260
280 LET B$(N)="?"
290 NEXT X
300 PRINT B$
310 INPUT C$
320 PRINT C$
330 IF A$(W)=C$ THEN GOTO 500
340 PRINT "SORRY. TRY AGAIN?"
350 INPUT C$
360 IF C$(1)<>"N" THEN GOTO 300
370 LET WR=WR +1
380 PRINT A$(W);"IS CORRECT."
```

```
390 LET A$ (W)=" "
400 PAUSE 120
420 GOTO 200
```

Statement 210 decides when the drill has gone on long enough. It is allowed to run for 20 words, no matter how many wrong or right answers. If you want the program to run for a longer time or a shorter time, just change 20.

Statement 220 selects the word. Notice that T, the variable that holds the size of the array A$, is used to determine the range of the random numbers.

Statement 230 is to allow for blank words in the array. If the randomly chosen array element doesn't have a word (which means that its code is less than the code for A), the program loops back to pick another random number.

Statement 240 transfers the word into another variable. The copy of the word in B$ will be altered. The original word is transferred intact and can be used again.

The **FOR/NEXT** loop contained between statements 250 and 290 is the core of the program. These statements randomly pick character positions within the word, then replace them with question marks (?). Statement 260 picks random numbers between 1 and 10. Statement 270 finds out if there is a letter at that space. Notice that the space could hold a blank, a letter, or a question mark. Both blank spaces and question marks have codes less than the code for A, so in either case, the program would loop back and pick another random number.

Statement 280 merely inserts a question mark in the chosen position.

The loop goes for R times. R is the number of characters to be replaced, as chosen by the person who typed the spelling words into the program.

The actual drill begins on line 300, where the word (with some letters replaced by question marks) is printed on the screen. The student types in an answer, which is compared with the original word. If they are equal, the student is correct, and the congratulatory display is invoked by the **GOTO** 500 command. Otherwise, the program announces that the choice was wrong, then invites the student to try again. If the student types anything beginning with an N (the program only looks at the first character—see the C$(1) in statement 360), 1 is added to the "wrong" score, and the program displays the correct spelling for the word for two seconds (**PAUSE** 120). The word is blanked out of the list to prevent frustration, and a new word is chosen.

If the student types anything else in response to the TRY AGAIN? question, the program loops back and prints the same word again. In all cases, the student's attempt is printed next to the test word, and all tries are displayed until the student moves on to another word.

The last section of the program controls the congratulatory display and also presents the score when the drill is over. Here are the statements:

```
500 FOR X=1 TO 10
510 LET N=INT (1+RND*20)
520 LET W=INT(1+RND*30)
530 PRINT AT N,W;"***YOU ARE RIGHT***"
535 PAUSE 10
540 PRINT AT N,W;
550 NEXT X
560 LET RT=RT+1
570 GOTO 200
1000 PRINT "RIGHT=";RT,"WRONG=";WR
```

The display given when the student gets a right answer runs from statement 500 to statement 550. In this loop, two random numbers are chosen, one between 1 and 20 and the other between 1 and 30. These are used in **PRINT** statements as **AT** locations. (The values 20 and 30 are to keep the message on the screen. The display actually has 21 rows and 31 columns.) Those numbers are then used to write ***YOU ARE RIGHT*** on the screen. Immediately after it is written, another **PRINT AT** statement writes over the message with blanks. This happens ten times, so that the message flashes and bounces all over the screen!

Once that is over, a 1 is added to the student's score, and the program goes back and chooses another word.

Once the program has gone through 20 trials, it jumps to statement 1000, prints the score, and finishes.

If you want to run it again without entering a new set of words, type the following commands:

```
LET; RT=0
LET WR=0
GOTO 200
```

If you have set the computer to **FAST** mode, you should also set it back to **SLOW** mode.

Using **GOTO** 200 instead of **RUN** leaves the variables intact. If you typed **RUN**, the array A$ would be destroyed, so you would have to type in the array again.

Note that the student will not be asked for words for which a wrong mark was given, since those words were blanked out. If you don't like that idea, deleting statement 390 will keep those words in the list. You could, in fact, modify the program to remove words that students got right; it's just a question of educational philosophy.

SCRAMBLED WORD SOLVER

Many newspapers feature scrambled word puzzles, in which you have to puzzle out an unknown word from a group of mixed-up letters (called an anagram).

This program will help: it takes the letters you enter, and randomly rearranges them. It will print new combinations of letters until you stop it. Here is the program:

```
10 PRINT "WORD?"
20 INPUT B$
30 LET L=LEN B$
40 LET N=1+INT (RND*(L-1))
50 LET C$=B$(L)
60 LET B$(L)=B$(N)
70 LET B$(N)=C$
80 PRINT B$+"";
90 GOTO 30
```

In response to the prompt "WORD?" you type in a string of letters. After you press **ENTER**, the program stores the number of characters in the word (**LEN B$**) in the variable L, generates a random number in the range of 1 to 1 less than the number of characters. The program then saves the last character in the word in C$, replaces the last character with the one in the randomly chosen position, and replaces the character in the randomly chosen position with the last character. Thus, the program switches one of the characters in the word with the last character. The program then exchanges the word, adding a space on the end to create a space between that word and the next, then loops around to exchange this new last letter with another one. Whew! Sound confusing? Don't worry, just run this program a few times and it will begin to make more sense to you.

This program is most helpful when the word is short. For example, when there are only 4 letters in the word, there are only 24 possible combinations. With 5 letters, there are 120 possible combinations. With 10 letters, there are 3,628,800 different arrangements for the letters. If you are trying to solve a long scrambled word, the most you can expect from this program is a suggestion of the right direction.

PLOTTING A SINE CURVE

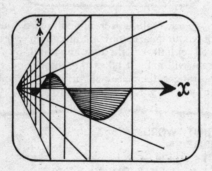

The **SIN** function produces the sine of a given angle. The angle must be stated in radians. You are probably accustomed to seeing angles in terms of degrees—there are 360 degrees in a circle. A circle contains 2π radians.

Anyway, here is the program:

```
10 FOR X=0 TO 2*PI STEP 2.1
20 PLOT 10*X,20+(10 SIN X)
30 NEXT X
```

A **FOR/NEXT** loop is defined with two separate statements: **FOR ... TO ... STEP** and **NEXT**.

FOR sets up a variable, called the loop counter, and gives it an initial value. The initial value is the first one after the equal sign. In statement 20, the inital value is 0. The **FOR** statement also sets up a **TO** value and a **STEP** value. All three values may be expressions, as you can see in statement 10. The expressions are evaluated as the **FOR** statement is executed.

After the **FOR** is executed, the program proceeds through the statements following it. In this case, the program expects line 20. The program proceeds until a **NEXT** command. The **STEP** value is then added to the initial value of the loop counter, and the computer checks to see if the counter variable's value is greater than the terminal value of the loop. If it is not greater, the program loops back to the statement immediately after the **FOR** statement, and performs that statement.

The program continues through the program's statements until it comes to the **NEXT** statement. Then it adds the **STEP** value to the counter variable, checks the counter variable, and, if the counter is still less than the terminal value, loops back. This process continues until the counter is greater than or equal to the terminal value. The loop is then finished, and the program proceeds with the statement after **NEXT**. In this case, once the **FOR/NEXT** loop is finished, the program ends.

If you don't give the **STEP** keyword and a **STEP** value, the default **STEP** value, 1, is used. If the **STEP** value is negative, the **TO** value *must* be less than the initial value. When the **STEP** value is positive, and the initial value is greater than (or equal to) the **TO** value, the loop is skipped.

POPULATION GROWTH

This program is an exercise in calculation. According to the *Global 2000 Report to the President*, the population over the next twenty years should grow at the rate of 1.8% a year.

This program calculates what the population will be in the future, assuming the present population at 4.5 billion and the continuing growth at the rate of 1.8% yearly.

The program will run indefinitely. When you are bored, press the **BREAK** key to stop it.

```
10 LET B=4500000000
20 LET Y=1982
30 LET Y=Y+1
40 LET B=B+.018*B
50 IF Y/100=INT (Y/100) THEN PRINT
   Y,B/1000000000; "BILL."
60 GOTO 30
```

FACTORIALS

One of the basic tools of probability is the factorial. In a sequence of linked events, the probability that any event will occur is related to the factorial of the total number of elements. A factorial is the multiplication together of all the whole numbers used to count up to the number in question. Thus, the factorial of 10 is 10*9*8*7*6*5*4*3*2*1, or 3,628,800.

For example, suppose you want to know how many combinations of the letters C, A, and N there are. If you put the letters down one at a time, there are three possible positions for the first letter you put down, two positions for the second letter you put down, and one position for the third letter you put down. Therefore, there are 3*2*1 or 6 possible arrangements. Here they are.

CAN ANC NAC ACN CNA NCA

This program finds the factorial of a number.

```
5 PRINT "GIVE NUMBER"
10 INPUT A
20 FOR X=A-1 TO 2 STEP -1
30 LET A=A*X
40 NEXT X
50 PRINT A
```

The FOR/NEXT loop starting in line 20 uses the loop counter X, which goes from one below the number down to 2. A FOR/NEXT loop can vary by any value, even by fractions. All you have to do is give the value in a STEP clause. X starts at a−1 because it is always multiplied by A. X goes down only to 2 because it is not necessary to multiply the number by 1.

A holds the total. Since its initial value is the number that was entered, it is not necessary for the loop to start with that number, but only with 1 below it instead.

Once the loop is finished, the answer is in A, and the program prints it.

10

Home Programs

CHECKBOOK BALANCING

This program will help you balance your checking account.

As we have stated before, when you decide to write a program, you must first plan exactly what the program is to do. Next, it's time to choose the BASIC language statements needed for the chosen task.

The first piece of information the computer will need to know will be your beginning balance. Next you'll want to enter the amount of each check or deposit. Finally, the computer should calculate and display the new updated account balance.

Here is a list of what the program should do:

1. Get account balance.
2. Get a check amount.
3. Any more checks to enter? If so, go back to 2.
4. If no more checks, print new balance.
5. Finish.

You have already seen the **PRINT** and **INPUT** statements. Using **INPUT**, your program gets the figure for the balance from the user. However, if you use only an **INPUT** statement, the person typing won't know what the computer is looking for. Therefore, it's necessary to use a **PRINT** statement before an **INPUT** to tell the person what to do.

```
100 PRINT "BALANCE?"
150 INPUT BAL
```

BAL is the variable used to hold the account balance. You could name the variable BALANCE, but the longer names require additional memory. You will find memory space to be a big problem, so you'll want to keep programs as short as possible; you'll often have to sacrifice some degree of clairity to gain a little extra memory space. You could have the computer print a longer message explaining what is wanted, such as PLEASE GIVE THE ACCOUNT BEGINNING BALANCE, WITH NO DOLLAR SIGN, but that would use up far more space than necessary. The use of shorthand names is perfectly acceptable, especially if you are the primary user of your programs.

You now have to enter the amount of the first check. Try typing in these three statements:

```
200 PRINT "AMOUNT"
250 INPUT AMT
300 LET BAL = BAL-AMT
```

After statement 300, BAL holds the new account balance.

Step 3 in the plan requires the program to find out if there are more checks to be entered. We must set up a rule that the program user types in an amount of 0 when there are no more checks, thereby terminating the program; this takes care of step 3.

```
350 IF AMT=0 THEN GOTO 500
400 GOTO 200
500 PRINT "NEW BALANCE IS $";BAL
```

Any number of items may appear in a **PRINT** statement. Each item is separated from the previous one by a comma (,) or a semicolon (;). Our program prints NEW BALANCE and, since there is a trailing semicolon, the value of the variable BAL is printed immediately on the same line.

Here is the entire program:

```
100 PRINT "BALANCE?"
150 INPUT BAL
200 PRINT "AMOUNT (ENTER 0 TO STOP)"
250 INPUT AMT
300 LET BAL=BAL-AMT
350 IF AMT=0 THEN GOTO 500
400 GOTO 200
500 PRINT "NEW BALANCE IS $";BAL
```

BUYING A HOUSE

Figuring out mortgage payments can be a bit painful with today's interest rates. You start off with a nice cottage, with a simple round price of, say, $100,000, at a simple interest rate of 20%. It all seems fairly clear, doesn't it? All right, where do you go from there? We, for one, could never understand how banks arrive at those equal monthly payments spread over thirty years. As you may have guessed, that's where this program comes in. (Incidentally, you can also use it to figure your car payments.)

To find out what the monthly payments on that cottage will be, just enter the appropriate figures when this program asks for them. Enter the loan amount where the program asks for HOUSE PRICE. Don't forget to subtract the amount of any down payment from the HOUSE PRICE you enter. The payment covers only the amount of the bank loan.

The total amount you will have paid is put in just to shock you. (Don't forget, you can deduct the interest from your income taxes.)

Here is the program:

```
10 PRINT "HOUSE PRICE?";
20 INPUT M
30 PRINT "$";M
40 PRINT "NUMBER OF YEARS?";
50 INPUT Y
60 PRINT Y
70 PRINT "INTEREST?";
80 INPUT I
90 PRINT I;"PERCENT"
100 LET I=I/100
110 LET PMT=M*I/((1+I)*(1−(1+I)**−Y))
120 PRINT "MONTHLY PAYMENT IS $";PMT/12
130 PRINT "TOTAL PAID IS: $";PMT*Y
```

SAVINGS PLAN

This program could also be titled "Planning for Retirement" or "The Truth about Your IRA Account." It computes the balance in your account, using your monthly savings deposit, interest rates, number of years, and, of course, inflation.

Here is the program:

```
10 LET T=0
15 LET D=0
20 PRINT "MONTHLY SAVINGS?";
25 INPUT M
30 PRINT "$";M
35 PRINT "NUMBER OF YEARS?";
40 INPUT Y
45 PRINT Y
50 PRINT "INTEREST?";
55 INPUT I
60 PRINT I;"PERCENT"
65 PRINT "INFLATION?";
70 INPUT INF
75 PRINT INF;"PERCENT"
80 FOR X=1 TO Y
85 LET YADD=0
90 FOR Z=1 TO 12
95 LET ADD=M-T*I/100/12
100 LET T=T+ADD
105 LET YADD=YADD+D
110 NEXT Z
115 LET D=D+YADD-(D+YADD)*INF/100
120 NEXT X
125 PRINT "TOTAL SAVED IS $";T
130 PRINT "AFTER INFLATION"
```

To use this program, just RUN it and answer the questions. The numbers you put in are "echoed" back to the screen, so you can see what you started with to arrive at the result. The echoing is done with the PRINT statements on lines 30, 45, 60, and 75. Note that the numbers are on the same line as the questions; this is accomplished by ending the PRINT statements containing the questions with a semi-colon.

The program uses the inflation rate you enter to calculate your money's real worth in today's dollars. The interest is compounded monthly, an arbitrary decision. If you want greater accuracy, alter the program by replacing the 12s in lines 90 and 95 with some other number (365 for daily compounding, 4 for quarterly compounding) or with a variable. If you use a variable, you would have to add another **PRINT** and **INPUT** sequence for the new variable. If you want to see in more detail how compounding is used, see the program for Calculating the Return on an Investment in this chapter.

Inflation is compounded only once a year, since that's how inflation figures are usually published. The difference in compounding periods makes the second loop necessary. If inflation was also compounded every month, the program would need only one **FOR/NEXT** loop.

This program takes quite a while to run. You may want to speed it up by running it in the **FAST** mode.

CONVERTING MEASUREMENTS

We once had a physics professor who insisted on giving problems in odd measurement. Furlongs-per-fortnight was his favorite. There is something in us that likes the normal American measurement system. The foot was set by the actual measure of a king's foot. An acre was the amount of land a person could plow in a day.

Romance is one thing, but converting measurements is another. We have never been able to remember how many tablespoons are in a cup, or teaspoons in an ounce.

Things get really complicated when you need to convert a recipe to feed more or fewer people. Our favorite cookbook recommends taking proportions with a method that we can barely figure out. If you have the same problem, this program is for you.

The program asks first for the number of servings in the original recipe, then the number of servings you require. If you are simply converting between measuring instruments (for example, you want to find out how many teaspoons of sugar equal one ounce), enter the same number for both the original and the number of servings.

The program then asks for the quantity you want to convert and the current units. The program looks only at the first two characters you type. It expects the first two characters of a unit name (CU, TA, TE, or OU). If it doesn't recognize your entry, it just asks again.

It then converts the measurements, finally displaying the new quantity in each of the four units. You are then asked if you have more to convert. If you answer YES, the program asks for another quantity to convert.

Here is the program.

```
1 PRINT AT 20,2;"****RECIPE CONVERTER****"
2 PAUSE 100
3 FOR X=1 TO 20
4 SCROLL
5 NEXT X
6 CLS
10 DIM Q$(2)
100 PRINT "ORIGINAL NUM OF SERVINGS?"
110 INPUT S
120 PRINT "NUM YOU WANT?"
130 INPUT N
140 LET N=N/S
150 CLS
160 PRINT "OLD QUANTITY:"
170 INPUT Q
180 PRINT "UNITS:"
190 INPUT Q$
195 CLS
200 IF Q$<>"CU" AND Q$<>"TA" AND Q$<>
    "TE" AND Q$<>"OU" THEN GOTO 180
210 IF Q$="CU" THEN LET Q=Q*48
220 IF Q$="OU" THEN LET Q=Q*6
230 IF Q$="TA" THEN LET Q=Q*3
240 LET Q=Q*N
```

```
250 PRINT INT (100*Q)/100;"TEASPOONS"
260 PRINT INT (100*Q/3)/100; "TABLESPOONS"
270 PRINT INT (100*Q/6)/100; "OUNCES"
280 PRINT INT (100*Q/48)/100; "CUPS"
290 PRINT AT 20,1; "MORE TO ENTER?"
300 INPUT Q$
310 IF Q$ < >"NO" THEN GOTO 150
```

Statements 1 to 6 provide a decorative beginning to the program. The **PAUSE** command momentarily halts the program. There are 60 **PAUSE** units in a second, so **PAUSE** 100 waits for 1.66 seconds. **SCROLL** erases the top line of the screen and moves everything up one line. The **CLS** command in statement 6 is needed because, after the **SCROLL**, the next **PRINT** statement appears at the bottom of the screen.

The program stores the original number of servings in the variable S and the new number of servings in the variable N, then divides N by S to get the conversion factor. Notice that the conversion factor is stored in N; reusing N saves an extra variable.

Statement 200 checks that the unit entered is acceptable to the program.

The length of Q$ is defined as 2 in a **DIM** statement on line 10. When the length of a string variable is defined in a **DIM** statement, the string variable will always have that length; therefore, all characters beyond the first two are totally ignored. For example, if CUPS was typed, variable Q$ would have the value CU, which is one of the legal values. If the user typed TBL instead of TABLESPOON, though, the program would not be able to handle the variable and would ask for another value for the unit.

Each of the **PRINT** statements on lines 250 to 280 includes an expression, **INT** (100*Q)/100. Q contains the converted number of teaspoons required. The rest of that expression ensures that only two characters will be printed to the right of the decimal point. It is assumed that a quantity such as 4.3567123 cups would not be of much help. The precision required by cooking should be satisfied by 4.35.

To simplify things, all of the quantities are converted to teaspoons before being processed. For the same reason, the new quantity is merely printed out in all four units. It would be possible to write a program to decide which unit was most appropriate.

Another useful program to have around is one that converts from English measurements to metric ones. It may sound hard, but it's really just like the recipe program above. You might even try to combine the two into a single all-purpose program. You use flatware in your kitchen, so why not software?

11

Business Programs

BALANCING YOUR BUDGET

Figuring your monthly budget can be a pain, especially if there are expenses to account for that are not billed every month. Some utility bills come every two months, for example.

This program is a very flexible, easily expandable budget calculating program. It can hold formulas for converting occasional expenses to monthly amounts. Within the memory capacity of your T/S 1000, you can expand this program to include just about anything you want.

Here is the program:

```
10 DIM E (5)
15 DIM M$(5,5)
20 DIM F$(5,8)
25 LET M$(1)="RENT"
30 LET F$(1)="E(A)"
35 LET M$(2)="UTIL"
40 LET F$(2)="E(A)/2"
45 LET M$(3)="CLOTH"
50 LET F$(3)=F$(1)
55 LET M$(4)="FD/WK"
60 LET F$(4)="E(A)*4.3"
65 LET M$(5)="OTHER"
70 LET F$(5)=F$(1)
100 PRINT "INCOME"
110 INPUT I
130 FOR A=1 TO 5
140 PRINT M$(A)
150 INPUT E (A)
160 CLS
170 LET E (A)=VAL F$ (A)
180 LET I=I−E(A)
190 NEXT A
200 FOR A=1 TO 5
210 PRINT M$(A);"=$"; E(A); "/Month"
220 NEXT A
230 PRINT "EXTRA=$";I
```

The secret of this program lies in understanding the function **VAL**. VAL, you will recall, evaluates a string as if it were a numeric expression. The string array F$ holds formulas for converting the numbers you enter into monthly equivalents.

For example, consider statement 40. F$(2) contains the string E(A)/2. E(A) is the number you enter for the amount of money you spent on utilities. A utility bill comes about every two months. Therefore, the formula F$(2) divides the bimonthly billing amount into a monthly equivalent. On the other hand, you figure food bills by the week. In order to convert that to a monthly amount, F$(4) multiplies E(A) by 4.3, since there are about 4.3 weeks in a month.

The loop that starts on line 130 prints an element from the M$ array, which contains messages identifying the budget categories, then gets values entered from the keyboard, putting them in the E array. Statement 170 converts the value using the formula from the F$ array. When the F$ array element is processed by **VAL**, it is just as if the string in that array element was right there in statement 170. For example, the second time through the loop, **VAL** F$(A) is equal to E(A)/2.

In fact, this program could have been written without a **FOR** loop. It would have been easy to write using a separate **PRINT**, **INPUT**, and conversion statement for each budget category. Writing the program with **VAL**, arrays, and a **FOR/NEXT** loop, however, saves space.

If you want to add more budget categories, all you have to do is change the size of the arrays, then put the appropriate strings in the next array elements. You will also have to change the **TO** values in the **FOR** statements.

For example, add the following lines to create a category for automobile expenses. (Some of these statements replace statements already in the program.)

```
10 DIM E(6)
15 DIM M$(6,5)
20 DIM F$(6,8)
80 LET M$(6)="AUTO"
90 LET F$(6)=F$(1)
130 FOR A=1 TO 6
200 FOR A=1 TO 6
```

Of course, you may have other expenses that we have left out. You probably have a telephone, for example, and you may have cable television. You may want to add categories for your laundry, for entertainment, and so on. Even if you have the basic computer with no additional memory, you should be able to add a few categories with no trouble. The elements of string array M$ might be made longer so that the messages are less cryptic. We kept the messages short so that the program would be small enough to make the job of adding categories easier. Once you have the program customized to fit your budget, you may want to make the program "friendlier" by making the messages more understandable.

CALCULATING INVESTMENT RETURN

When our bank started compounding the interest on our savings accounts daily, we stopped trying to figure out anything. How much would we have in five years? Who knows?

This program starts with a fixed amount of money, a fixed interest rate, and a fixed compounding rate, then calculates the value the original investment will be worth, each year for the number of years you request.

Here is the program:

```
100 PRINT "AMOUNT?"
110 INPUT A
120 PRINT "NUMBER OF YEARS?"
130 INPUT Y
140 PRINT "INTEREST OR APPRECIATION?"
150 INPUT I
160 PRINT "NUMBER OF TIMES COMPOUNDED"
170 PRINT "PER YEAR"
180 INPUT C
190 CLS
200 FOR X=1 TO Y
210 FOR Z=1 TO C
220 LET A=A+A*I/C/100
230 NEXT Z
240 PRINT "YEAR";X;"$";A
250 NEXT X
```

Lines 200 and 210, respectively, start two **FOR/NEXT**

loops. These are "nested" loops, that is, one is completely contained inside the other. The outer loop represents years. The inner loop is the number of times per year the interest is compounded.

If a loop begins after another one starts, the second loop must be nested inside the first. In other words, since **FOR X** comes before **FOR** Z, **NEXT** Z must come before **NEXT** X. Once the inner loop is initiated, that loop is allowed to complete its cycling before the computer proceeds to search for the **NEXT** statement belonging to the outer loop. If the computer reaches the **NEXT** statement for the first loop before reaching the **NEXT** statement for the second loop, it will lose track of where it is supposed to go in the program. In any case, your program wouldn't work the way you expected, if at all. So, either make sure your loops are completely independent, or nest them carefully.

Another interesting line in this program is line 220:

220 LET A=A+A*I/C/100

This formula is supposed to calculate the new principle after adding interest. The part that represents the interest is I/C/100. This assumes that you enter the interest as a percentage. For example, when you are asked to supply INTEREST OR APPRECIATION, if the interest on your account is 17%, you should enter 17. Interest is the percentage increase added to your account each year. Percentage is a number taken out of 100. Therefore, to get, for example, 17% of $1,000, simply multiply $1000 by 17 and divide by 100. The variable C is in the formula I/C/100 because that is the number of times the interest is compounded each year. When your bank compounds your interest, it figures out how much interest you earn for the compounding period and adds that to your account. If you earn 17% interest, compounded once a year, on a $1,000 deposit, $170 will be added to your account at the end of the year. If your interest is compounded every three months, $42.50 is added to your account in the first quarter, $44.31 in the second quarter, $46.19 in the third quarter, and $48.15 at the end of the year. The total for the year is $181.15. The difference is that, when the interest for the second quarter is calculated, you are paid interest on the interest you made in the first quarter, and so on.

To use this program, just enter your beginning account balance, the number of years you want, the interest rate (enter a number, without a percent sign—if you are expecting 5% interest, enter a 5; if you expect 5 1/4%, enter 5.25), and the number of times the interest is compounded per year. The program will list the value of your investment at the end of each year. If the investment is compounded many times a year, the program will run quite slowly. Speed it up by using the **FAST** mode. Also, if you specify a period greater than 22 years, the program will stop because the screen will fill. In that event, you can type **CONT** to clear the screen and get the remaining years.

Here's an exercise to try with this program. The Federal Reserve claims it takes about two days to clear a check. One of the largest banks in the country holds funds on checks for a minimum of six days. Thus, they have the use of depositors' money for the extra four days. During that time, they don't let it just sit around; they lend it, probably at about 16% interest. Suppose the bank had a million customers, each one with an average of $100 waiting to clear at any given time. That gives the bank $100 million to lend at the prime rate every day. Run the program (in **FAST** mode), and enter a principle of $100,000,000, for a period of one year, 16% interest, compounded daily. (Don't enter either the $ or the %.)

Your program should come up with about $17 million profit. And you've always wondered why it takes a week to clear a check from around the corner!

A BETTER CALCULATOR

This program is about as simple as a program can be, yet it is, in some ways, better than your calculator. Before getting into what it does, here is the program:

```
10 INPUT A$
20 PRINT A$;"=";VAL A$
30 GOTO 10
```

When you run this program, you get a pair of quotation marks at the bottom of the screen. All you do is enter any mathematical expression and then press **ENTER**. The computer gives you back your equation, along with the answer. The expression can be as long as you like, but can only use constants, functions, and operators. For example, you could use the following expressions:

```
SIN 1
2**3−8*7
3*RND
```

The **VAL** function calls the expression evaluator to evaluate the formula that you have entered.

The program's great advantage over a calculator is its ability to give you back the expression you started with, along with the answer. Thus, you can see if you've made a mistake in typing. A calculator doesn't have this feature.

The program is terminated by entering an illegal numeric expression—a letter, for example.

GENERAL RECORD-KEEPING

This program keeps notes, lists of bills paid, lists of tax deductions, lists of charges, or any kind of records you choose.

It is very simply structured in order to reserve the greatest amount of space for actual records.

The program has three possible operations. It can add records, review the records that have been saved, or save itself onto tape. Each function is separated into a distinct section.

Here is the program, but don't try to run it until you've read this whole discussion—it won't work without some "initialization."

```
10 PRINT "ADD,REVIEW,SAVE"
20 INPUT B$
30 CLS
40 GOTO 100*CODE B$
3800 PRINT "RECORD:"
3810 INPUT B$
3820 LET A$=A$+B$+"**"
3830 GOTO 10
5500 FOR X=1 TO LEN A$
5510 IF A$(X)<>"**" THEN PRINT A$(X);
5520 IF A$(X)="**" THEN PRINT
5530 NEXT X
5540 GOTO 10
5600 SAVE "RECORDS"
5610 GOTO 10
```

Line 10 prints the "menu" of possible actions. Statement 20 accepts the chosen action. (You can type in the full word or just the initial letter.)

Statement 30 clears the screen once a new action is chosen. This prevents confusion and saves memory space. Based on your chosen number, the expression 100*CODE B$ is a compact way to sort out which routine was chosen. Every character has a different internal code, and the CODE function returns the code for the character you input. The code for A is 38, the code for R is 55, and the code for S is 56. Therefore, the program will jump to statements 3800, 5500, or 5600 depending on the letter entered. Notice that the program does not check for an invalid answer. If you type in something beginning with a letter besides A, R, or S, the program may not do what you want.

The section for adding records is from line 3800 to 3830. It asks first for a record, then accepts the string in B$. In order to save space, the menu variable is reused to hold the string. The program then takes the old value at A$, adds the new record onto the end, then adds a double asterisk (**). The double asterisk should be entered with the double asterisk key. A$ now contains all the old records, plus the new record, with a ** on the end. The ** is used to distinguish between records and is used by the next section of the program. If a dash, for example, were used to separate records, the computer would mistake a dash inside one of your records for a record separator, and the record would be stored incorrectly.

The review section of the program runs from statement 5550 to statement 5540. It uses a **FOR/NEXT** loop to run through A$, from position 1 to the end (**LEN A$** gives the total length of A$). Line 5510 tests each character to see if it is a double asterisk. If not, the letter is printed. Notice that the line ends with a semicolon (;). That instructs the computer to print the next item on the same line, immediately after the previous item. Statement 5520 also checks to see if the current character is a double asterisk. If it is, that statement executes a **PRINT** statement, so that the next character printed goes at the beginning of the next line. This breaks the records up so that each one begins on a new line. When a double asterisk is found, it signals the end of a record. The double asterisk, of course, is never printed.

The last section of the program, lines 5600 and 5610, are invoked if you enter **SAVE** in response to the menu. Statement 5600 saves the program onto tape; to do this, get your tape recorder ready, start it running, and then enter S (to **SAVE**) in response to the menu. Since the program is saved while it is running, when you **LOAD** the program off tape, it starts running right away. Statement 5610 is executed first, and the program jumps back to the menu. (For a discussion of this process, see Chapter 5.) After the **SAVE** instruction has been executed, the program goes back to the menu. You can then continue using it, or get out of the program. To get out, **DELETE** the left quote mark which is on the bottom of the screen, and type **STOP**. You can also simply type a T, U, V, W, X, Y, or Z. The **GOTO** statement will cause the program to jump to the nonexistent line number, and the program stops.

If you have tried to **RUN** this program, you will have found that it will not work. If you begin by trying to add a record, the program fails on statement 3820, because A$ is on the right side of the **LET** statement, and it hasn't been defined yet. To run the program, you have to type the following commands. (Note that they don't have line numbers.)

```
LET A$=""
GOTO 10
```

(The two quotes are two **SHIFT**/P's, not one **SHIFT**/Q.)

Never use **RUN** to execute this program. **RUN** clears all variables and will destroy all records you have put into the program. Use **LET** A$="" only the first time you put records into the program. If you use **RUN** after you have saved records, those records will be destroyed. If you save the program onto tape using the S instruction to the menu, you should never have to start the program running again, anyway.

It is a good idea to use a different copy of the program for different types of records. Since the memory space in your computer is limited, you don't want to try to squeeze too much into one copy of the program. Moreover, it will be easier to find specific information if you have stored information by type. To make a fresh copy of the program for a new type of record, load an old copy. Stop the program and enter the **LET** and **GOTO** commands shown before. You will now be starting with an empty copy of A$. When your magazine service tells you that you owe them money, you can tell them that your computer says that you have already paid.

This program, as it's currently written, has one great shortcoming: you cannot remove any of the records. To remedy this shortcoming, add the following routine:

```
5521 IF A$(X) ="**" THEN INPUT B$
5522 IF B$ < >"REMOVE" THEN GOTO 5530
5523 LET B$=A$ (X+1 TO)
5524 LET X=X-1
```

```
5525 IF A$(X) < > "**" THEN GOTO 5524
5526 LET A$=A$ (TO X)+B$
5527 GOTO 10
```

When you use the review function with this routine in the program, the program waits for string input after each record is printed. If you type **ENTER** (or anything but RE-MOVE), the next record is displayed. If, however, you type REMOVE, the program stores the rest of the string in B$. (Once again, B$ is being reused to save an extra variable.) Notice the "slicing" command used: A$ (X+1 TO). The X position has the current double asterisk, so X+1 points to the beginning of the next record. The phrase X+1 TO refers to the entire string from the beginning of the next record to the end.

Once the information is safely stored in B$, lines 5524 and 5525 search backward in A$ for the double asterisk immediately in front of the unwanted record. When the record is found, line 5526 changes A$ to contain the records from the beginning to the double asterisk in front of the deleted record (A$(TO X)) and the contents of B$. Since B$ contains everything in A$ beyond the deleted record, the deleted record is sliced out of A$, leaving everything else intact.

Statement 5527 jumps back to the menu. You may well wonder why the delete routine doesn't allow the review loop to continue. Since the record was sliced out of A$, A$ is now shorter; the termination value of the **FOR/NEXT** loop, however, was set by the original length of A$ and cannot be changed without starting the loop over again. It would be possible to save the value of A$ at the time of interruption, then start the loop again with the new length of A$, but that would take a new variable or two and several program lines—and all that takes up memory space. If you purchase the memory extension, you will probably want to make these changes. Since the space is needed to store additional records, it is better just to go back to the menu and start reviewing from the beginning again.

This program illustrates a general method of storing records. You could store each record in an individual element of a character array, but that would almost certainly take more space, because the array elements would have to be a standard size. By storing records in a string, they are stored in the minimum amount of memory. By separating the records with a standard character, the computer can tell when each record is finished. This method (known as *variable length record indexing*) is very similar to the methods used by sophisticated computer systems to store data.

TELEPHONE BOOK

This is not much of a "program," in that you never **RUN** it, but it isn't a bad address book.

The program is composed of as many sets of the following two lines as necessary.

```
5 PRINT "NAME", "TELEPHONE NUMBER",
   "ADDRESS"
10 STOP
```

Your address book would consist of as many such sets as necessary to hold all the numbers you want. For example:

```
5 PRINT "FBI", "(415) 556-6600",
   "SAN FRANCISCO, CA"
10 STOP
15 PRINT "ASIAN ART MUSEUM",
   "(415) 558-2993", "GOLDEN GATE PARK"
20 STOP
25 PRINT "MAYOR", "(415) 558-3456",
   "CITY HALL"
30 STOP
```

This list is accessed by **GOTO** commands. So that you don't have to remember all those numbers—how long would you remember that 5 is the FBI, 15 is the Asian Art Museum, etc.?—use **LET** commands to store the line numbers in variables with easily remembered names. For example:

LET FBI = 5
LET ASIAN ART = 15
LET MAYOR = 25

You could store the line numbers in more than one variable name if you have trouble remembering them. For example, EFRAM= 5 might be easier for you to remember.

In order to use the list, all you have to do is enter a command like this:

GOTO MAYOR

The computer prints the contents of the **PRINT** statement on line 25 and then the program stops.

If you save this program on tape, all the variables will also be saved. Remember never to type **RUN** or **CLEAR** when the program is loaded, or you will wipe out the variables and have to reload the program.

This program has the disadvantage that each line number variable can hold only a single line number; if you have two friends with the same name, you will have to use a different variable name for each. This is a problem for people who have trouble remembering last names and index their ordinary address books by first names: the J page has a dozen Johns and Joes. This problem can be solved by making the computer display every entry under a given letter. This would display all the J's at once, and you could pick the one you wanted. In that case, though, you won't have to alphabetize all the names.

The following telephone book program is much more complex, but gets around the problems of the simpler one.

The program presented here has four functions: you can add entries to the address book, change entries, look at entries in the book, and save the program on tape.

This program automatically saves itself onto tape while it is still running. When you load it from tape again, it continues to run. If you stop the program, use a **GOTO** 30 command to restart it, or you will destroy all the data.

Before we discuss how this program is structured, here it is:

```
1 LET K=0
10 DIM A$(10, 25)
20 DIM B$(1)
30 PRINT "ADD, CHANGE, REVIEW, SAVE"
40 INPUT B$
50 CLS
60 GOTO CODE B$*100
3800 LET K=K+1
3820 IF K>10 THEN GOTO 30
3830 LET E=K
3840 GOTO 6000
4000 PRINT "ENTRY NUM"
4010 INPUT E
4020 IF E>0 AND E<11 THEN GOTO 6000
4030 GOTO 30
5500 PRINT "KEY"
5510 INPUT B$
5520 FOR X=1 TO K
5530 IF A$(X,1) = B$ THEN PRINT X;"";A$(X)
5540 NEXT X
5550 GOTO 30
5600 SAVE "ADDRESS"
5610 GOTO 30
6000 PRINT "NEW ENTRY"
6010 INPUT A$(E)
6020 GOTO 30
```

This isn't a very long program, but it does quite a lot. There are some tricks that keep it short.

One note about the array A$, defined in statement 10. As the program is written here, it can only hold ten names and phone numbers. With additional memory, it will hold many more. If you want to include street addresses, you must either increase the length of each element of the array or use some kind of shorthand that you can easily understand.

The first point of interest is the way that the program chooses the action routine. Look at statement 60:

60 GOTO CODE B$*100

All computers use numbers to represent letters. That internal representation is called a *code*. **CODE** is a function that gives the code for a string character. **CODE** only gives the code for the first character of the string that it is given. The variable B$ is dimensioned to 1 to conserve space, since nothing the user types beyond the first character matters anyway.

Since **GOTO** can use an expression in place of a constant line number, the expression used in line 60 directs the program with only a single statement. Notice that there is no protection against an unexpected answer. If the user enters something besides A, C, R, or S, the program will probably fail.

So the rest of the program consists of five routines, each of which does one simple thing. The first four routines begin with line numbers determined by the code of the first character of the user's entry.

The ADD routine begins with line 3800. The variable K is used to remember the last part of the array that was used. Each new entry is written in the first available empty space in the array. When the array is full, the ADD request is rejected by line 3820, with no message. If memory space were not so much of a problem, we could tell the user explicitly that there is no more space in the array. As it is, the user must guess what happened. The only clue is that the program stops asking for a new entry. You will certainly want to correct details of this sort when you have more memory.

On line 3830, the number of the first empty array element is transferred into the variable E. Line 3840 then causes a jump to line 6000, which is the beginning of the fifth routine.

The routine on line 6000 simply adds a new entry. This routine always uses the variable E to define the location of the new entry. If the user is changing an entry, E is the number of the entry to be changed.

The CHANGE routine begins on line 4000. It first asks for an entry number. (The review routine prints an entry number along with the entry. The user who wishes to change an entry must first use review to find out the entry number, and then use CHANGE to alter the contents of the entry.)

Finally, the REVIEW routine begins on line 5500. It first asks for a *search key*. A search key is merely a string used to search for some particular piece of data. In this case, the program goes through the array and compares your key with the first character in each element. When a match is found, the program prints it. For example, if you enter a key of J (the key can only be one letter), the computer prints all entries that begin with J.

The fourth routine simply saves the program. After you have added entries, you should position your tape, start the recorder running, type S, and press **ENTER**. The program and all its data are stored on the tape. As always, it is a good idea to save the program at least two or three times, in case something happens to one copy. Once the first SAVE is finished, the program will come back to line 30 again, so you can just enter another S without turning the recorder off. When you load it from tape, the loaded version will continue from line 5610, so that line 30 will execute immediately.

APPENDIXES

APPENDIXES

A

Accessories

A cassette tape recorder is probably the first accessory that you will want for your Timex/Sinclair 1000. For many people, a cassette recorder is almost a required piece of equipment, saving much frustration. Cassette recorders are discussed in Chapter 5.

A large number of other accessory devices are available; accessories that attach directly to a computer are called *peripherals*. This list, beginning with the more useful and generally available accessories, is not exhaustive, but covers most of the types of equipment you can attach. Prices mentioned are for reference only. For more information, check the ads in computer magazines, the store where you bought your computer, or other computer and electronics stores.

PRINTERS

A printer is a very important accessory. It will print out anything that your TV screen can display.

The printer sold by Timex uses rolls of heat-sensitive paper about 3½ inches wide. Similar printers are available from other companies. There may be other compatible printers that will print on ordinary paper, but we don't know of any at this time.

Installing the printer is easy: just plug the printer into the slot on the back of your Timex/Sinclair 1000.

There are three print commands. **LPRINT** works exactly like the **PRINT** command. To print your program on the printer instead of the screen, simply replace the **PRINT** statements with **LPRINT**. **LPRINT** prints one line (32 characters) at a time. It prints out after every 32 characters or after a **PRINT** statement that does not end with a comma or semicolon. (If you use **LPRINT** statements when you do not have a printer connected, the computer may not work. If this happens, you can restore normal operation by pressing the **BREAK** key.)

The second printer command, **LLIST**, acts exactly like the **LIST** command, except that the printer is used instead of the TV.

The third command, **COPY**, copies whatever is displayed on the screen onto the printer.

MEMORY EXTENSIONS

The Timex/Sinclair 1000 comes with slightly over 2,000 bytes of memory. A *byte* is a small piece of information, equivalent to a single character. One thousand bytes are referred to as one kbyte, or simply, one K. The standard Timex/Sinclair 1000 has 2K of memory.

As you use this machine, you will quickly discover that 2,000 characters are not a very large memory. You may run out of memory if you are writing a complicated program or if you are writing a program that stores information. The telephone book programs in Chapter 11, for example, will use up a 2K memory very quickly.

An additional 16K of memory are available for about $50 from Timex and a number of other suppliers.

There are no special considerations for using extended memory. Programs are written the same as for a smaller amount of memory, but the computer will now hold more program lines. With additional memory you do not have to watch the size of your programs as carefully; this means you can write friendlier and more easily understood programs. For example, the **REM** command, virtually ignored in this book, may be used to leave notes to yourself in programs. **REM** lines are ignored by the computer and are simply an aid to the user. The programs in this book don't use **REM** statements because they are a luxury when there is so little memory available. For longer programs, **REM** statements are a necessity.

More memory also permits using longer variable names. In order to save space, this book almost always uses one-letter variable names. When you have extra memory, you can use longer, more meaningful variable names.

The upper limit for program space is 16K of memory, but companies besides Timex sell 32K and 64K memory packages. The additional memory may be used to store program data and variables.

BATTERY PACKS AND POWER SUPPLIES

Occasionally, you may want to use your computer when no AC current is available. (During a blackout, for example, or while hiking through Tibet.) If so, a battery pack is just for you.

A battery pack that can power your computer for from thirty minutes to two hours costs between $40 and $90. Battery packs also help regulate AC line current when you are using normal AC. If the power drops quickly, the voltage regulator inside your Timex may have trouble dealing with the change and your computer could crash. If you find that your computer crashes at the same time your lights dim, a battery pack would cure the problem.

Other types of power supplies are available for as much as $50. If you add several accessories to your computer, you may find that the standard power supply is not adequate, and a separate power supply may be required.

INPUT/OUTPUT BOARDS

An input/output (or I/O) board is an electronic device that controls communications between a computer and the outside world. I/O boards enable you to connect your Timex to peripherals built for other computers: other kinds of printers, disk drives (see the entry later in this appendix), character readers, card readers, bar-code readers, and many other devices. You can also use I/O boards to connect your Timex to another computer.

In addition, I/O boards are available for controlling household lights, a burglar alarm system, or even a robot.

TELEPHONE MODEMS

A modem (modulator/demodulator) allows your computer to communicate with another computer over a telephone line. If you have a modem, you can connect to a wide range of computer services, including news, stock market reports, and "electronic shopping." Modems will probably be available through Timex, but many other companies offer them now. Prices for modems start at close to $100.

SPEECH AND SOUND BOARDS

Speech and sound boards allow your computer to produce simulated speech and (real) music, by playing computer signals through a loud speaker. Usually one board will not produce both types of sound, since the sound in speech is quite different from the sound in music. You can also buy voice recognition units, which may cause your computer to respond to your voice. Be aware, however, that voice recognition technology is not very far advanced at the moment.

COLOR BOARDS

Boards are available for use with color televisions. The forthcoming Timex/Sinclair 2000 will have a color board.

TYPEWRITER-STYLE KEYBOARDS

The weakest feature of the Timex/Sinclair 1000 is the flat, tiny keyboard. Replacement keyboards that look and feel much more like regular typewriters cost about $50. Such a keyboard will improve ease of use and accuracy. The Timex/Sinclair 2000 will have an improved keyboard. Be careful—many replacement keyboards are sold that require a great deal of work to install. Make sure you buy one that just plugs in.

DISK DRIVES AND OTHER MASS STORAGE DEVICES

A device such as a cassette recorder is known in computer parlance as a "mass storage" device since it stores so much more than the computer's internal memory. An ordinary cassette recorder has two limitations. The first is that it is slow. It takes almost a minute to load or save a program. The second problem is that you must set up the tape for the computer.

The least expensive way to solve at least one of these problems is a specialized type of cassette recorder, sometimes called a stringy-floppy. This is a tape recorder that uses an endless-loop tape, which loops around so you never have to press REWIND; the computer can start and stop the tape, and control whether the cassette is on playback or record. A stringy-floppy, including hardware for computer control of the tape, sells for about $100.

A disk drive is a much faster storage device that stores information on a round platter coated with a magnetic film similar to that found on tapes. Disk drives are usually expensive. The least expensive kind (the only kind that you might sensibly hook up to a Timex/Sinclair 1000) uses a flexible disk that comes in a cardboard or plastic case. These flexible disks, often called floppies because you can bend them, range in size from 3 inches in diameter to 8 inches. They are fast and easy to use, and cost between $3 and $5 each. However, the floppy disk drive costs a minimum of several hundred dollars. It is rumored that a floppy disk drive will eventually be available for the Timex/Sinclair 1000 for about $100.

JOYSTICKS

If you play a lot of games, joysticks may add to your fun. Joysticks, a common accessory on home video games, are available for the T/S 1000. These devices allow the cursor to be moved rapidly about the screen.

OPTICAL BAR-CODE READERS

Bar-code scanners read the bar codes that have recently appeared on everything from books to candy. Optical readers of this type are used primarily for data entry. You may have seen a bar-code reader used at supermarkets or other stores.

EXPANSION BOARDS

If you are interested in developing your own hardware for the Timex, whether for your own purposes or for sale, an expansion board may be a good idea. This expands the amount of access you have to the I/O port on the back of the Timex/Sinclair 1000, giving you more room for work.

OTHER DEVICES

There are a number of other useful devices available. Light pens let you instruct the computer by "drawing" on the TV screen. Real-time clocks (sometimes battery-powered) let you "time" programmed events. A quick tour through the pages of computer magazines may reveal additional peripherals you never even dreamed of.

B

Computer Anatomy

COMPUTERS AND HUMANS

A computer may be compared to the human body. It has a brain, ears, means of speech, a heart, and a circulatory system.

The human brain consists of two main parts: the part that does the thinking and the part that remembers things. The Timex/Sinclair 1000's brain has a Z80A microprocessor for calculating: when you ask your computer to add two numbers, the calculating is done by the microprocessor. The microprocessor wouldn't be any good if it couldn't remember which two numbers it was supposed to add, so it also has memory.

The computer also has a means of communicating with you. You tell the computer what to do by using the keyboard; when you touch a key firmly, the computer sets the message. You can attach wires to the antenna jacks of your television, and the computer will display what you type on the keyboard, plus its own messages.

The computer's "circulatory system" pumps electricity. The Timex/Sinclair 1000's "power supply" takes the electricity running through the walls of your home and converts it so that the computer can use it.

Any computer, large or small, has the same five essential parts: a processor that does the thinking, a memory that saves pieces of information for the processor, a keyboard, a display, and a power supply.

ACCESSORIES

Anything put into the memory of your Timex/Sinclair 1000 remains there until you change it or turn the computer off. A cassette recorder will eliminate the pain of retyping programs. Chapter 5 tells you how to use a cassette tape recorder with your T/S 1000.

A cassette recorder is an almost essential accessory. A printer is also useful for keeping a permanent copy of data.

Memory extensions are available for the Timex/Sinclair 1000. When you store programs on a cassette recorder, you can reload them back into the computer; but the computer can retain only a limited amount in its memeory at any given time. You can increase the amount it can remember at one time with a memory extension.

HARDWARE AND SOFTWARE

What we've described so far—the physical parts of your computer, the parts you can actually touch—are called the hardware of the system.

A simple hand-held calculator consists only of hardware. Theoretically, you could take your calculator apart and touch the part that does addition, the part that does division, and so on.

A computer program, on the other hand, is intangible. You could not take the computer apart and touch a piece of a "checkbook balancing program." This is because computers are run by sequences of steps that tell the computer what to do. One step might be "Get the beginning account balance," followed by a step that said, "Get the first check amount."

These sequences of steps are programs. Programs are called *software* to show they are different from the hardware that makes up the physical computer.

It is software that really makes a computer different from a calculator. A calculator is capable of a fixed set of actions. A computer is capable of performing many different tasks. When you want your computer to do something new, you can just load in new software, (as long as the hardware can do what is required).

Every computer has a program, or group of programs, called the *operating system.* When you use your Timex/

Sinclair 1000 to do arithmetic, the operating system tells the hardware how to do the calculation you requested. Also, when you type on the keyboard, the letters appear on the television screen because the operating system puts them there.

MORE ABOUT MEMORY

Although the software makes your computer run, the hardware determines just how much the software can do. You could, for example, try to write a program to make your computer walk around. (If you do, patent it quickly.) Timex/Sinclair 1000s can't be made mobile because they just don't have the hardware to do it. Similarly, there is a limit to just how many instructions you can load into your Timex/Sinclair 1000.

The operating system that comes with the computer is permanently locked into part of the computer's memory. There is nothing you can do to change it, move it, or damage it. It is kept in a special kind of memory that can only be read, but not written on. This type of memory is called *read only memory,* or ROM. You are probably familiar with cartridge-based video games. If you want to play a different game, you just pull out the old cartridge and slip in a new one. The cartridges actually contain ROM. The video game machine is a special-purpose computer, and the ROM in the cartridge is a program, just like a program for a game in the local arcade.

If your Timex/Sinclair 1000 contained nothing but ROM, it would be no better than a game-cartridge machine. What makes the Timex/Sinclair 1000 a multipurpose computer is its memory, which you can change. You can write your own programs, type in programs, get programs from magazines, or buy them on cassettes.

This kind of memory is called *random access memory,* or RAM. It is called random access memory because it can be either read from or written to, as required. You don't have to go through a program step by step. At any time, you can access any part of a program. Therefore, you are free to move *randomly* around the memory that stores the program.

C

Resources

PUBLICATIONS
FOR TIMEX/SINCLAIR COMPUTERS

HEURISTICS (schematics, etc.)
25 Shute Path
Newton, MA 02159

SYNC (magazine)
39 East Hanover Ave.
Morris Plains, NJ 07950

SYNTAX (newsletter)
The Harvard Group
RD2, Box 457
Harvard, MA 01451

COMPUTER MAGAZINES
OF GENERAL INTEREST

BYTE Publications Inc.
70 Main St.
Peterborough, NH 03458

CREATIVE COMPUTING
P.O. Box 789-M
Morristown, NJ 07960

PERSONAL COMPUTING
Hayden Publishing Co.
50 Essex St.
Rochelle Park, NJ 07762

HARDWARE SUPPLIERS FOR
TIMEX/SINCLAIR COMPUTERS

BYTE-BACK CO.
Rt. 3, Box 147
Brodie Rd.
Leesville, SC 29070

C.A.I. INSTRUMENTS
2559 Arbutus Ct.
Midland, MI 48640

CUTS CO.
P.O. Box 37
Mamaroneck, NY 10543

DATA-ASSETTE
56 South 3rd St.
Oxford, PA 19363

E-Z KEY
Suite 75
711 Southern Artery
Quincy, MA 02169

KOPAK CREATIONS INC.
448 West 55th St.
New York, NY 10019

L.J.H. ENTERPRISES
P.O. Box 6305
Orange, CA 92667

MEMOTECH CORP.
7550 Westyale Ave.
Suite 220
Denver, CO 80227

MICRO ACE
1348 East Edinger
Santa Ana, CA 92705

MICRO DEVELOPMENTS
Box 1140
2000 Center St.
Berkeley, CA 94704

MINDWARE
15 Tech Circle
Natick, MA 01760

RKL SYSTEMS
P.O. Box 515
Leominster, MA 01453

SINCLAIR RESEARCH
LTD.
3 Sinclair Plaza
Nashua, NH 03061

TIMEX COMPUTER COR-
PORATION
Waterbury, CT 06720

WALSH & SIMMONS INC.
2511 Iowa St.
St. Louis, MO 63104

SOFTWARE SUPPLIERS FOR
TIMEX/SINCLAIR COMPUTERS

A. LONG ACRE
546 Leitch Ave.
Skaneateles, NY 13152

BANI-TECH
P.O. Box 1568
Princeton, NJ 08540

BANTA SOFTWARE
Rd. # 7
Bethlehem, PA 18015

COSMONICS
Box 10358
San Jose, CA 95157

DETRON OF HAWAII
2007 Naio St.
Honolulu, Hawaii 96817

FREE GOODIES LIST
P.O. Box 3073
San Jose, CA 95156

FUN WARE
7119 Santa Fe Ave.
Dallas, TX 75223

GLADSTONE ELECTRON-
ICS
901 Fuhrmann Blvd.
Buffalo, NY 14203

H & H ELECTRONICS
3379 Route 46-6D
Parsippany, NJ 07054

HENSLY
Box 334
Asheboro, NC 27203

LAMO-LABORATORIES
Box 2382
La Jolla, CA 92038

MICRO ACE
1348 East Edinger
Santa Ana, CA 92705

MINDWARE
15 Tech Circle
Natick, MA 01760

NEW ENGLAND SOFT-
WARE
Box 691
Hyannis, MA 02601

N G M INC.
P.O. Box 18701
Oklahoma City, OK 73154

NIRAD ELECTRONICS
959 East 460 South
Provo, UT 84601

ROMAN SOFTWARE
788 Mercury Circle
Littleton, CO 80124

SINCLAIR RESEARCH
LTD.
3 Sinclair Plaza
Nashua, NH 03061

SOFTSYNC INC.
P.O. Box 480
Murray Hill Station
New York, NY 10156

SOFTWARE APPLICA-
TIONS
P.O. Box 1922
Atascadero, CA 93422

SYNCHRO-SETTE
388 West Lake St.
Addison, IL 60101

TIMEDATA
3 Waldon Rd.
Califon, NJ

TIMEX COMPUTER COR-
PORATION
Waterbury, CT 06720

RICHARD TOY
546 CR 214
Fremont, OH 43420

TOM WOODS
Box 64
Jefferson, NH 03583

ZETA SOFTWARE
P.O. Box 3522
Greenville, SC 29608

USERS' GROUPS AND RESOURCES FOR TIMEX/SINCLAIR COMPUTERS

Arizona

Randy Saxton
4827 N. 63rd Ave.
Phoenix, AZ 85033

California

PERKIN-ELMER USERS'
GROUP
Rein Smith
8333 Pumalo
Alta Loma, CA 91701

Dr. George Kuby
P.O. Box 34534
Los Angeles, CA 90034

George Mockridge
263 Gateway #107
Pacifica, CA 94044

William Madden
P.O. Box 8201
Sacramento, CA 95818

Robert Jorgenson
3814 Coleman Ave.
San Diego, CA 92154

HIGH SCORE VIDEO AR-
CADE
Marc Reiniz
2301 Mission St.
Santa Cruz, CA 95060

STANFORD TELECOM-
MUNICATIONS, INC.
Paul Perrault
1195 Bordeau Dr.
Sunnyvale, CA 94086

Colorado

Cap Hamilton
767 S. Gaylord St.
Denver, CO 80209

Washington, D.C.

WASHINGTON AREA
USERS
P.O. 6239
Washington, DC 20015

Florida

SPACE COAST
MICROCOMPUTER CLUB
Bruce Hosken
70 Darwin Ave.
Merritt Island, FL 32952

SAM-BAM USERS'
GROUP
Mel Routt
P.O. Box 596
Safety Harbor, FL 33572

NO SUNCOAST FL
PASCO-HERNANDO
USER'S GROUP
John Dowland
P.O. Box 5021
Spring Hill, FL 33526

Georgia

ATLANTA ZX80/81
USERS' GROUP
Phil Hoffstadter
P.O. Box 2842
Atlanta, GA 30301

Iowa

Jim Carroll
1218 William St.
Iowa City, IA 52240

Idaho

I. W. (Will) Underwood
P.O. Box 1195
Idaho Falls, ID 83401

Illinois

CHG AREA HOBBYIST
EXCHANGE SPEC INT
GRP
Larry Weigel
323 S. Franklin #804
Chicago, IL 60606

CIRCLE CHESS GROUP
A. F. Standis
P.O. Box 63
Des Plaines, IL 60017

Diana Wright
2170 Oak Brook Circle
Palatine, IL 60067

Indiana

SINCLAIR MIDWEST
USERS' GROUP
Robert C. Carroll
P.O. Box 13042
Fort Wayne, IN 46866

Andrew Thomas
2804 E. 55th Pl., Suite Q
Indianapolis, IN 46220

FUN-Z
W. Long
P.O. Box 914
Jasper, IN 47546

Louisiana

Tom Fussell
13721 Chef Menteur
New Orleans, LA 70129

GULF COAST SINCLAIR
USERS' GROUP
144 Terry Dr.
Slidell, LA 70458

Maryland

WESTINGHOUSE ELEC
CORP ADV TECHNOLO-
GY LABS
Jack Fogarty
Box 1521
Baltimore, MD 21203

PRINCE GEORGES SIN-
CLAIR USERS' GROUP
Jim Wallace
5448 Tilden Rd.
Bladensburg, MD 20710

SEABROOK/LANHAM
SINCLAIR USERS' GROUP
Cora C. Dickinson
9528 Elvin Lane
Lanham, MD 20706

Massachusetts

MITRE BEDFORD
SINCLAIR/TIMEX COMP.
CLUB
Ed Lindsay
Box 208, E170 Mail Stop
Bedford, MA 01730

BOSTON COMPUTER SO-
CIETY
Sue Mahoney
3 Center Plaza
Boston, MA 02136

Michigan

MICHIGAN AREA USERS'
GROUP
Lance M. Ward
433-D E. Edgewood Blvd.
Lansing, MI 48910

Minnesota

Tom Lindquist
1740 Beechwood Ave.
St. Paul, MN 55116

Missouri

Carlos Colon
1228 Pitcher
Joplin, MO 64801

North Carolina

John Drummond
P.O. Box 12546
Research Triangle Park,
NC 27709

North Dakota

K. Allen Ward &
Lonnie Misner
520 Tulane #205
Grand Forks, ND 58201

Nebraska

Patrick Murphy
4903 Walker
Lincoln, NE 68504

New York

ZX USERS OF AMERICA
Michael Wilson
626 Water St.
New York, NY 10002

ZX USERS' GROUP OF
NEW YORK
Box 650
Wall St.
New York, NY 10005

UPPERSTATE NEW YORK
ZX81 USERS
Vern Olsen
13 Dennis Ave.
Plattsburg, NY 12901

Pennsylvania

USERS' GROUP OF CEN-
TRAL PA
Bill Russell
RD 1, P.O. Box 539
Centre Hall, PA 16828

PGH AREA COMP CLUB
SPEC INT GRP—SIN-
CLAIR
Dick Welsh
1605 Middlecrest Dr.
Glenshaw, PA 15116

Tennessee

CHATANOOGA AREA
SINCLAIR USERS
Dan Williams
P.O. Box 1321
Collegedale, TN 37315

William Tracey
3220 Lakeland Dr.
Donelson, TN 37214

Jimmie Barker
3791 Barron Ave.
Memphis, TN 38111

Utah

Quint B. Randle
255 N. 1600 W. #76
Provo, UT 84601

Virginia

Jim Langston
146 Hawthorne Dr.
Newport News, VA 23602

CENTRAL VIRGINIA
USERS' GROUP
Herb Miller
Rt. 1, Box 192
Troy, VA 22974

Washington

Jeff Pack
21026 109th SE #708
Kent, WA 98031

Dan Gallery
1619 E. John St. #414
Seattle, WA 98112

PROGRAM EXCHANGE
17058 28th NE
Seattle, WA 98155

West Virginia

SINCLAIR SUPER GROUP
William Meclaw
949 Brier St.
St. Albans, WV 25177

Wisconsin

Robert C. Harris
5827 N. Maitland Ct.
Milwaukee, WI 53217

D

Glossary

absolute value. The positive value of a number, regardless of its sign. For example, the absolute value of −5 is 5, just as the absolute value of +5 is 5.

argument. The argument of a function is the value that the function operates upon to produce the desired result. For example, if you type **PRINT** PEEK 1200, you are telling the computer to look (PEEK) at the location in memory identified by the address 1200 and to **PRINT** what it finds there. In this example, PEEK is the function, and 1200 is its argument.

array. A group of related variables (called elements) that all go by the same variable name; you create all the elements of an array with a single **DIM** statement and access them with the variable name followed by subscript.

array element. Any of the variables that make up an array. See *array*.

BASIC. Beginner's All-purpose Symbolic Instruction Code. The language used on the T/S 1000, and the most widely used microcomputer language in the world.

bug. An error in your program that causes an unsuccessful execution.

byte. A byte represents one character of information to the computer and consists of eight binary digits, or bits of information.

command line. The program line you create at the bottom of the screen is considered the command line, until you **ENTER** it.

command mode. When you type a statement and **ENTER** it without a line number, it is considered a direct command because it is executed immediately. This is called command mode, or immediate mode. Statements entered without line numbers are destroyed upon execution and do not become part of any program listing.

conditional clause. A clause within a statement that, if true, will result in one course of action being taken or, if false, will result in another. In an **IF . . . THEN** statement, the **IF** portion constitutes a conditional clause; if true, the **THEN** portion of the statement will be executed; if false, the program continues at the next line number.

constant. An item whose value remains fixed throughout program execution. Numbers are good examples of constants.

crash. This is just a little bit of computer slang to impress your friends with; if your program crashes, it simply means that it failed to execute properly. Usually the cause is an error, or bug, in your coding.

current line. In a program listing, the line containing the current line pointer. By pressing **SHIFT/EDIT**, the current line can be copied to the bottom of the screen, where it can then be edited as desired.

current line pointer. In a program listing, the arrow that appears at the beginning of the program line that is immediately available for editing. By use of the **SHIFT**/6 (down arrow) and **SHIFT**/7 (up arrow), any line can be selected as the current line, which can then be edited.

cursor. The cursor, appearing in the lower left-hand corner of the screen, is the computer's way of saying it is ready to accept your commands. The location of the cursor is the location where the next entered item will appear on the screen. When you wish to delete an item from a line, the cursor is always directly to the right of the position(s) that will be affected when you press **SHIFT/DELETE**.

debug. To find and eliminate the errors in a program. Debugging is an important part of successful programming.

dimensional string variable. The variable name used in a string array, which must be defined as a string variable followed in parentheses by the number of strings in the array, and the length of each string. For example: **DIM A$(10,8)**. See *array*.

echo. A character that appears instantaneously on the screen when you type it on the keyboard is an echo.

exponentiation. The process of raising a number to a power of itself. For example, using exponentiation, you can express 10*10*10*10*10 as 10**5 (ten to the fifth power). Expressing large numbers by using exponentiation enables you to conserve memory space.

expression—See *numerical expression*.

expression handler. A program built into the T/S 1000's memory that evaluates numerical expressions and computes their value.

F cursor. Accessed by pressing **SHIFT/ENTER**. When the F cursor is displayed, the computer expects the next entry to be a function. After the function has been entered, the F cursor is replaced by an L cursor.

functions. Special programs, permanently stored in the computer's memory, which perform selected mathematical operations. The functions are printed below the keys and can only be invoked when the F cursor is displayed.

G cursor. Accessed by pressing **SHIFT/9**. The appearance of the G cursor indicates that the computer will accept graphics characters. The G cursor is removed from the screen by again pressing **SHIFT/9**.

graphics mode. The graphics mode enables you to type inverse characters as well as graphics characters. The graphics mode can only be entered by typing **SHIFT/9** and can only be exited by typing **SHIFT**/9. When the computer is in the graphics mode, the **G** cursor is displayed.

immediate mode—See *command mode.*

infinite loop. Within a program, a loop that, once entered, will continue indefinitely, until the user stops execution of the program. An infinite loop should never intentionally be written into a program.

integer. A whole number; a number expressed without added fractions or decimals. Zero (0) is also an integer, as are negative whole numbers (such as −5).

inverse characters. Normally, your computer prints black characters on a white (or light) background. In the graphics mode, however, you can print inverse characters, which are white on a black background. This can only be accomplished with the **G** cursor on the screen (**SHIFT**/9).

K. Kilo, or thousand. In computer terminology, 1K stands for 1,024 bytes. The T/S 1000 has a built-in RAM of 2K, or 2,048 bytes, and a ROM BASIC of 8K or 8,192 bytes.

K cursor. Appears at the beginning of every new program statement. It signals to the user that the computer is awaiting a keyword. Entering a keyword replaces the **K** cursor with an **L** cursor.

keyword. A keyword tells the computer what type of command you are giving it. A keyword is expected at the beginning of every program statement and can only be entered when the **K** cursor is displayed.

L cursor. When the **L** cursor appears on the screen, you may enter letters and numbers, plus the period and space. You cannot enter keywords, functions, or graphics characters while the **L** cursor is displayed.

line number. The number you assign at the beginning of each program statement. Line numbers identify the lines in your program; the computer automatically puts your program statements into ascending numerical order according to their line numbers.

literal—See *string.*

loop counter. A numeric variable, the value of which is incremented or decremented by the step value every time the loop is executed, until the termination value of the loop is reached.

loop variable—See *loop counter.*

nested loop. A loop that is fully enclosed within another loop. Whenever more than one loop exists within a program, each loop must either be independent of the others or fully nested. No loop should begin inside of another loop and end outside of it.

numerical expression. Two or more numbers joined by an operator. With the exception of line numbers, you may use numerical expressions anywhere you need to express numerical values. Examples of numerical expressions include 1=1; 2*5; 9—3/2; and 4**7.

numeric variable. A variable used to contain numeric data only. Numeric variables' names may be any length of alphabetical and numeric characters, the first of which must be a letter.

operator. Any of the five operators the computer will accept in numerical expressions: + (addition); — (subtraction); * (multiplication); / (division); ** (exponentiation). Remember, the double asterisk (**) used for exponentiation must be obtained by keying in **SHIFT**/H, not by typing **SHIFT**/B twice.

print position. The location of the next item to be printed. The print position can be controlled from your program by the use of features such as **TAB**, **PRINT AT**, **PLOT**, and **UNPLOT**.

program. A series of instructions that causes the computer to perform a specific task. Your list of program lines, or statements, makes up the program.

program line. A command line preceded by a line number becomes a program line once you **ENTER** it. Program lines are not executed by the computer until you give the command to **RUN** the program.

program statement—See *program line.*

RAM. Random access memory. A type of memory that can be both written into and read from. The contents of RAM undergo a constant state of change as a result of program execution. Also known as read/write memory.

relational expression. A mathematical expression of the relationship between two items on either side of a relational operator. The six valid relational operators are $>$, $<$, $=$, $>=$, $<=$, and $<>$. A relational expression will always be either true or false.

report codes. Numbers that appear in the lower left corner of the TV screen, separated by a slash, indicating why the program has stopped executing. A report code of 0/300 tells you that the program ran successfully (0) and that line number 300 was the last one executed. The report code also assumes the role of the K cursor, so that keywords may be entered when a report code appears on the screen. Also known as internal status messages. (For a complete list of report codes, see the back of the *T/S 1000 User Manual*.

ROM. read only memory. Memory that is preprogrammed by the manufacturer so that it can be read from but cannot be written to, or altered by, the user.

string. Anything you enclose within quotation marks is called a string. Strings are not evaluated by the computer; they are taken at face value and given no special significance. When you **PRINT** a string, the quotation marks surrounding it are dropped. To use quotation marks within a string, you must type **SHIFT/Q**, which produces a set of double quotation marks; they will appear as single quotation marks when you **PRINT** the string.

string constant—See *string*.

string expression. Strings connected by the addition (+) operator. String expressions may contain both string variables and string literals. For example, **LET** A$="ABC" +B$ is a valid string expression.

string literal—See *string*.

string variable. A variable that is used to hold a string. Must be named with a single letter (A–Z) followed by a dollar sign ($). For example, A$, B$, C$, etc.

variable. A symbolic name that may assume different values at various times during the execution of a program.

E

Report Codes

Every time the Timex/Sinclair 1000 performs a command or
stops execution of a program, it prints a report code on the
bottom line of the TV screen. These codes are of the form:

number1/number2

Number2 is a line number. If this code is displayed after
performing a command, the line number is always 0. If the
number is displayed after a program has been run, the number is the last executed line number of the program.

Number1 is a report code that indicates why command or
program execution stopped.

A report code of zero means that the command was successfully completed. If you had run a program, the 0 means
that the computer simply ran out of lines to execute. If you
stopped the program with a **STOP** command, you will get a
report code of 9, or sometimes D. Stopping the program
with the **BREAK** key yields a report code of D.

Other report codes indicate that the computer had some
kind of problem in attempting to execute your command or
program.

There are a total of 15 possible report codes: 0 – 9, A, B, C, D, and F. (There is no report code E.) Here are the report codes and their meanings:

Code	Situation	Meaning
0	After any action	No problem encountered.
1	**NEXT** statement	The loop counter named in the **NEXT** statement has not been used in a **FOR** statement, but there is an ordinary variable with the same name.
2	An undefined variable has been used.	A variable must have a value assigned to it by an **INPUT** or **LET** statement before you can use the variable anyplace else (except in a **DIM** statement). An array has to be defined in a **DIM** statement before you can use it.
3	Array or string with a subscript	The subscript you save was too large for the array or string, or was equal to 0. (If the subscript is too large ever to use with any variable or array, you will get error B.)
4	Any situation	There is no room left in memory. When this occurs, the report code may be incomplete. For example, the code may say 4/, with no line number. This means that your program simply does not have room in which to execute, or the command you gave does not have

Code	Situation	Meaning
		room to execute. Be aware that what is written on the TV screen takes up substantial memory. If the screen is full, more than a third of memory is taken up just by the screen. Use **CLS** to clear the screen and free that memory. Erasing a line by using a **PRINT** statement does not free up any memory; it just replaces the line with blank spaces. (If you are using the optional extended memory package, the data for the display always takes up the maximum amount of space, so **CLS** does not free up any memory.)
5	The screen is full.	Press **CONT** to clear the screen and continue the program where it left off. You can also give the **CLS** command and **GOTO** any line number, or forget about the program and give any command.
6	Any arithmetic operation	You have somehow gotten a number larger than the computer can handle. Numbers cannot be larger than about 10^{38} (positive or negative).
7	**RETURN** statement	A **RETURN** statement was executed without a corresponding **GOSUB**.

Code	Situation	Meaning
8	**INPUT** used as a command	**INPUT** may be used only in a program statement. (That is, **INPUT** must have a line number before it.)
9	**STOP** command was executed.	The execution of a **STOP** command may have ended a program, or **STOP** may have been entered as a command. This is not an error.
A	The argument to **SQR, LN, ARC-SIN (ASN)**, or **ARCCOS (ACS)** was invalid.	The arguments to these functions have to be in specific ranges. For example, you cannot find the square root (**SQR**) of a negative number.
B	The argument for certain functions and commands was too large or too small, or was negative.	Functions and statements that require integer arguments always round the argument off to the nearest integer. If the resulting number cannot be handled by the command or function, this error occurs.
C	**VAL** function was used with an invalid argument.	The **VAL** function evaluates its argument, which must be a string, as if it were a numeric expression. You get this error if you use **VAL** on a string that is not a valid numeric expression.
D	**BREAK** or **STOP** used as a command (not in a program statement to stop a program)	You can stop a running program with the **BREAK** key, or, if the program asks for input, by giving the **STOP** command. If

Code	Situation	Meaning
		you do so, the program will end with this report code.
F	Tried to **SAVE** a program without giving a program name.	You must give a name in a string following a **SAVE** command. The name can be a blank space or a single letter (although neither is a particularly good choice), but you must not enter a null string. (If you try to give a **SAVE** command without any string following, the line will be rejected with a syntax error.)

F

Troubleshooting

Computer malfunction can take many forms. The computer might simply refuse to show its initial prompt, it could refuse to show the characters and keywords you type in, it could refuse to understand your commands, or it could refuse to perform your commands. Here are some suggestions for finding the problem.

Is the computer installed correctly? Check the instructions in Chapter 1 of this book. If the cursor is displayed on your TV screen, this probably isn't the problem. If you have a blank screen (not covered with snow, but an even blank grey screen), it is possible that the vertical hold of your TV is out of adjustment.

Is the power supply plugged into a working socket? Perhaps you have blown a fuse. It may be hard to believe, but many, many calls to large computer repair services are about problems resulting from a faulty socket, a blown fuse, or a plug pulled out.

Is there something wrong with the TV? Try connecting the computer to another TV.

Is the computer overheated? If you leave your computer in direct sunlight, it may stop working.

Is there some kind of radio interference? It is possible (but highly unlikely) that radio signals may interfere with your computer's operation. Is there a ham or CB or commercial radio antenna nearby? Try moving the computer to another part of your house.

Is one of the cables faulty? The best clue to this is intermittent operation. If it seems that your computer is running fine, and then it stops working when you move it a little, the cables may be at fault. If your computer always refuses to work, it might still be the cables.

Still no good? Try calling the store from which you bought the computer and asking for suggestions. Finally, call Timex or send the computer to their service center.

INDEX